ADRIAN ROGERS

REVELATION
STUDY GUIDE
Volume One

innovo
PUBLISHING

Published by Innovo Publishing, LLC
www.innovopublishing.com
1-888-546-2111

innovo
PUBLISHING

Providing Full-Service Publishing Services for
Christian Authors, Artists & Ministries: Hardbacks, Paperbacks, eBooks,
Audiobooks, Music, Film & Courses

Revelation Study Guide (Volume 1)

LOVEWORTHFINDING®
WITH ADRIAN ROGERS

Unless otherwise noted, all scripture quoted is
from the King James Version (KJV) of the Bible.

ISBN: 978-1-61314-492-3

Cover Design & Interior Layout: Innovo Publishing, LLC
Printed in the United States of America
U.S. Printing History
First Edition: 1998
Second Edition: 2019

CONTENTS

ABOUT DR. ADRIAN ROGERS
AND
LOVE WORTH FINDING

Known for his evangelistic zeal and uncompromising commitment to the Word of God, Adrian Rogers was one of the greatest preachers, respected Bible teachers, and Christian leaders of our time. For over fifty years, he consistently presented the Good News of Jesus Christ with strong conviction, compassion, and integrity.

Under his pastoral leadership, Bellevue Baptist Church in Memphis, Tennessee, grew from 9,000 members in 1972 to more than 29,000 at his retirement in 2005. And Adrian Rogers was a leader in his denomination, serving three terms as president of the Southern Baptist Convention.

In 1987, Adrian Rogers founded Love Worth Finding Ministries to broadcast and publish God's truth around the world through radio, television, print, and now online. Love Worth Finding can be heard in more than 150 countries, and continues to provide Adrian Rogers' messages around the clock.

These study guides are straight out of Adrian Rogers' messages and will provide hope, clarity, love, and truth as you study God's Word.

ABOUT THIS STUDY GUIDE

To help you delve deeper into God's Word and learn step-by-step how to apply His principles to your life, Love Worth Finding offers this study guide. It is ideal for family devotions, neighborhood Bible studies, or Sunday School, as well as for your own personal study. To assist you in using the study guide, each lesson is broken down into sections:

Overview
The Overview gives a capsulated thought to set the scene for the lesson.

Introduction
The Introduction provides a concise snapshot of the passage being studied.

Discussion
The Discussion summarizes Dr. Rogers' teaching on the material covered in each lesson and provides a basis for continued study.

Application
The Application section contains questions designed to challenge the reader to look deeper into the biblical text and to find answers with practical application to life. This section is especially helpful when using the series for small group study.

Digging Deeper
Digging Deeper pulls together the message of the lesson and adds more insight, often elaborating on items of historical or cultural relevance.

REVELATION
INTRODUCTION

The book of the Revelation offers the believer a dramatic overview of the end times, from the rapture of the church to the very end of the age.

The apostle John was called away from fishing by Jesus Christ, became His best friend, and watched the ministry of the Lord develop. He was there on the mount of transfiguration, in the garden of Gethsemane, and at the foot of the cross of Calvary. Some of the last words Christ spoke in this world were to John, asking him to take care of Jesus' mother, Mary.

John became a fearless preacher of the gospel, a leading evangelist and pastor in the early church; and a sensitive writer of God's Word. He penned the fourth gospel, and three letters he wrote to young believers are part of the holy canon of Scripture. Yet at the end of his life, John was exiled to the barren island of Patmos by Caesar for preaching the truth of the gospel. While "in the Spirit on the Lord's day," John heard the voice of God calling him to heaven, where he was shown the events that would lead to the end of the world. He wrote the things the angel told him to, and his vision offers us a clear look on the end times.

THE IMPORTANCE OF REVELATION

The Revelation is the only book that guarantees you a blessing if you will only read it: "Blessed is he that readeth," John writes in Revelation 1:3, "And they that hear the words of this prophecy, and keep those things which are written therein; for the time is at hand."

It is like the clasp which binds the volume of the Bible together. Genesis describes the start of this world, and Revelation explains the end. If Genesis is the seed-bed of all theology, then Revelation offers the fruit of all theology. It completes the pictures begun by the Old Testament prophets, and gives details that clarify the prophecies of Daniel, Isaiah, and Ezekiel. As you study the vision given to John, other texts will become clear, and you will begin to see the pattern and plans of God throughout history. If you ignore the Revelation, you will be left to wonder at the events of the world, without any knowledge of the prophetic word concerning things to come.

THE CENTRAL TRUTH OF REVELATION

The book of Revelation is a unique work. The language seems different, and the images incredibly vibrant, but one message comes through loud and clear: Jesus Christ is coming again. He is coming back. The first time He came as Savior, but the next time He will come as Sovereign. The first time He came humbly, and died on the cross as a suffering servant. Even though the Old Testament prophets foretold the birth of the King, most people on earth missed it.

But when Christ comes back, no one will be able to miss it. He will return in power, and in glory, and in majesty. He will defeat Satan and his armies, wipe sin from the face of the earth, and set up His eternal kingdom. The book of the Revelation details all of the events surrounding the second coming of Jesus Christ, and provides the believer with joyous hope for the future and powerful motivation for holy living in the present.

Chapter 1

THE BLESSING BOOK

OVERVIEW

God's primary purpose in giving Revelation was to forewarn and to bless His people.

INTRODUCTION • REVELATION 1:1-3

In the Book of Revelation, we see the completion and fulfillment of the work that God began in the Book of Genesis. If Genesis is the seed-bed of all theology, then Revelation is the fruition of all theology; Revelation is the golden clasp which binds the volume of the Bible together.

The parallels between these two books are many. For example, in the Book of Genesis, the first man, Adam, reigns on the earth. In Revelation, the last Man reigns in heaven in glory. In Genesis, the darkness and the seas are created. In Revelation, there is no more darkness nor any sea. In Genesis, a bride, Eve, is presented to her husband. In Revelation, the church is presented to her husband, the Lord Jesus Christ.

In the Book of Genesis, we see the tree of life in the Garden of Eden. In the Book of Revelation, we see the tree of life in God's new creation. In Genesis, the beginning of sin brings death and a curse. In Revelation, sin is done away with; there is no more curse and no more dying. In Genesis, Satan appears to man for the first time. In Revelation, he appears for the last time.

In the Book of Genesis, man is driven from the garden and from God's presence. In the Book of Revelation, man sees God's face again in glory. In Genesis, men look for a city by faith. In Revelation, the holy city is presented to men in glory. In Genesis, Satan utters the first lie ever heard: "Ye shall not surely die" (Genesis 3:4). In Revelation, there is a city where liars will never enter.

It is important to see the Books of Genesis and Revelation in comparison and in contrast with one another. What God began so long ago at the first creation, He will ultimately complete in His new creation.

DISCUSSION

Jesus Christ Revealed

The central person of the Book of Revelation is not John (as the title may lead you to believe), but Jesus Christ. This is a revelation of Jesus as told to John. If we study the Book of Revelation and don't learn anything about Christ, then we've misread the Book of Revelation.

The word *revelation* comes from the Greek word *apocolupsus* which means "unveiling" or "uncovering." Revelation is meant to be an unveiling of the Lord Jesus Christ, much in the same way that a beautiful sculpture is unveiled and viewed for the first time.

Revelation is meant to be an unveiling of Christ to us, but it also tells of the time when Christ's glory will be unveiled, or revealed, to all people. When Christ came to us the first time, His glory was veiled. When He comes again, His glory will be completely unveiled.

Savior and Sovereign

Jesus' second coming as shown in the Book of Revelation is going to be very different from His first coming when His glory was veiled. Jesus first came to be crucified; He will come again to be crowned the King of Kings. When He first came,

He stood before Pontius Pilate to be judged; when He comes again, Pilate will stand before Him to be judged. Jesus first came to endure shame; when He comes again, He will come in splendor. He came first to redeem; now He is going to come to reign. The first time, Jesus came as a suffering servant. When He comes again, He will come as the mightiest sovereign of all.

We must see Jesus both as He is in the Gospels and as He is in the Book of Revelation. Otherwise, we will not know the fullness of Christ. We need to know Him not only as Savior, but also as Sovereign. We must see Jesus not only as the Justifier, but also as the Judge. Jesus is our Redeemer, but He is also our Ruler. One of the purposes of Revelation is to reveal these aspects of the Lord Jesus Christ.

The One Who Is Coming

When studying the Book of Revelation, it is very easy to become focused on trying to decipher and understand the prophecy. However, our main focus is to be on the One whose coming is prophesied. After all, it's not the coming we want to be familiar with, but the Person who is coming.

Here is a good illustration. Imagine a train station. In the train station is a station master whose main objective is to know as much as possible about all of the trains. And he has all kinds of intricate charts to help him predict exactly where a train is and when it will reach the station. Imagine also that there is a young lady at the station. She is not nearly as well-informed as the station master, but she knows that her fiancé is on the train that is about to arrive, and she can hardly wait for it to get there.

I hope that in your study of Revelation, you will be like the young lady whose heart beats in anticipation of the arrival of the one she loves. You may find a justification for your point of view, or you may find reasons to support some point of doctrine. But if you don't find Jesus in the Book of Revelation, you have missed the real point.

The Things to Come

Not only does the first verse of Revelation tell is who the central Person of the book is, it also clearly explains the purpose of the book. The revelation of Jesus Christ was given to John "to show unto his servants things which must shortly come to pass."

God's purpose in giving us this book is to show us, His servants, certain things about the future. Only God has the knowledge and the authority to do that. Contrary to what others may claim, no other being, whether fleshly or spiritual, has knowledge of the future.

For Bond-Slaves Only

The word translated in Revelation 1:1 as *servants* is the Greek word *douloi*. It literally means "bond-slaves." Anyone who seeks to understand Revelation must be willing to be a bond-slave to Christ, for these are the people for whom this prophecy is intended—people in full submission to Him.

Both Sure and Near

There are two characteristics of this prophetic vision to which Revelation 1:1 calls our attention. First, the prophecy is certain to happen; these are things which must come to pass. Just as Old Testament prophecy was fulfilled in the first coming of Christ, so the prophecies concerning His second coming are to be fulfilled. There were many who missed out on the blessing of His first coming because they did not believe the prophecies really would be fulfilled. But they were: Christ was born of a virgin in Bethlehem just as the prophets foretold.

The other important characteristic of Revelation is that the events described in it are near; these things must shortly come to pass. Of course, *shortly* does not mean "momentarily," because nearly two millennia have passed since John wrote about this vision. Rather, *shortly* means "suddenly" or "with out warning." In the twinkling of an eye these things will come to pass (1 Corinthians 15:52). That is why Jesus repeatedly tells us to be ready.

Signs and Symbols

Another piece of information we find in Revelation 1:1 is the way in which God reveals this message to His servants: "He sent and signified it by his angel."

Much of what is in Revelation is signified, or revealed, through symbolism. These symbols will be studied in greater detail later in this series. What is important to know at this point is that the key to understanding the symbolism of Revelation is a good understanding of the rest of Scripture. Many symbols are allusions to things that happened in the Old Testament.

Because of the symbolic nature of Revelation, questions arise as to whether certain parts of it are to be interpreted symbolically or literally. But a proper understanding of Revelation requires both. For example, Revelation 12:3-4 describes Satan as a great red dragon having a tail that could sweep one-third of the stars out of heaven. That is obviously a symbolic description, but it does not mean that Satan himself is not a literal being. The characterization of Satan as a dragon shows his ferocity and power. The stars represent angels that chose to follow him and fell from heaven. This is a symbolic representation of Satan, but it is to be believed quite literally.

The Comforting Promise

In Revelation 1:3 we find a promise of great comfort to believers: "Blessed is he that readeth, and they that hear the words of this prophecy, and keep those things which are written therein: for the time is at hand." Not only must we read what God has sent to us, but we must also heed, or take to heart, what it says. If we do, then God will bless us. That is His special promise to us.

The promised blessing is the second coming of Jesus Christ. Revelation foretells that the days leading up to His coming will be marked by war, economic disaster, natural disaster, and societal decay. But we who know God's Word can take heart, because we know that Christ's coming is near. And when He comes, He will finally bring everlasting peace and righteousness to the world (Zechariah 9:10). So as you study Revelation, take to heart its prophecy and its words of comfort.

The Certain Prophecy

The final truth we will look at in this passage is the last part of Revelation 1:3 "The time is at hand." Again, "at hand" does not indicate immediacy, but imminence. The things prophesied in this book can happen at any time, and they will happen without warning. That is another aspect of the blessing to those who read and heed Revelation—they will be prepared. The time of preparation is now, because as 1 Thessalonians 5:1-3 says, these times will come upon us like a thief in the night.

Six Signs of the Times

So the things that are prophesied are imminent, and they will come to pass without warning. When Jesus' disciples asked Him when the appointed time would be, Jesus replied that He did not know—only the Father in Heaven knows the day and the hour (Matthew 24:36). However, Revelation does foretell some signs of the times. I believe that there are six major signs that show the time is truly at hand.

1. The establishment of the modern State of Israel. In May of 1948, the Jewish people returned to their land for the first time in almost 2,000 years. I believe this re-birth of Israel is what Jesus referred to in Matthew 24:32-33 and that this is one of the most significant signs of the end times our generation has seen.

2. Russia's rise to prominence as a major world power in the twentieth century. Ezekiel 38:15-16 refers to a mighty power coming out of the north, which will eventually come against Israel. Bible scholars believe this refers to what is today the Commonwealth of Independent States—the former Soviet Union.

3. The revival of the Roman Empire. Revelation 17 and Daniel 2 both describe a great, fallen empire that rises again and is reborn. That empire is believed to be Ancient Rome, which will be reborn as a ten-nation confederacy. It is possible that the ten-member European Common Market is that confederacy. Out of this empire will come the Antichrist.

4. The rise of occultism and demon worship. First Timothy 4:1 says, "in the latter times some shall depart from the faith, giving heed to seducing spirits, and doctrines of devils." In Europe, there has been a sharp increase in the practice of witchcraft. In America, our bookstores are filled with books on witchcraft, astrology, black magic, transcendental meditation, and all kinds of occult practices. They are calling it "New Age," but it's the same old spirit of demon worship, and it is being taught in our public high schools. Meanwhile, prayer has been banned from the classroom in the name of separation of church and state.

5. The increase of earthquakes. In the last few years, we have witnessed the terrible destruction of earthquakes all over the world—in North America, in Asia, and in

Europe. Jesus warns in Matthew 24:7 that the last days are going to be marked by an increase in earthquakes.

6. Famines and pestilence. These are also foretold in Matthew 24 and in Revelation 16:1-11. You only have to read the evening paper to see how many areas of the world are suffering from the worst famines and plagues of disease in decades.

All of these truths will be dealt with as we go through this series; this chapter is only meant to be an introduction. But throughout our study of Revelation, we will see that one recurring theme is inescapable: The time is at hand. The sands of time are running out for this generation, and the time for reconciliation with God is now.

APPLICATION

1. How would you describe your attitude toward the Book of Revelation? Have you always considered it to be a "book of blessing"? Why or why not?

2. Read these passages: Genesis 2:8-10, 17-19, and 23-24. Compare the outlook for mankind in these passages with that in Revelation 22:1-5. How will God restore to us what we have lost?

3. Who is the "main character" in the Book of Revelation? Who, according to Revelation 1:1, sent the revelation to John? What does this tell us about Christ's relationship to us?

4. Read the description of Jesus in Isaiah 53:1-9. Compare this with the picture of Him in Revelation 19:11-16. Why do you think so many people didn't accept Jesus as the promised Messiah when He came the first time?

5. There is one "main event" foretold in Revelation around which all the other events in this Book revolve. What is it? According to the following passages, what should our attitude be toward this event?

   1 Corinthians 1:7

   1 Thessalonians 5:23

   Titus 2:11-13

6. For whom is the Book of Revelation intended? How might it be interpreted by those who are not in submission to God? (1 Corinthians 2:14)

7. Can you think of some reasons why God often uses signs and symbols to reveal truths to us? Who else did this and why? (Luke 8:10)

8. Based on what has already been revealed to us through the rest of Scripture, is there any reason to believe that the events of Revelation might never happen? (Read Amos 3:7 and Ephesians 1:9-10.)

9. Many people avoid studying Revelation because they feel it is difficult to understand and not particularly relevant to day-to-day life. Evaluate this attitude in the light of these Scriptures:

   Proverbs 8:34

   Matthew 7:24-27

   2 Peter 3:11-14

10. List the ways that Jesus described what the day of His coming would be like:

Matthew 24:27

Matthew 24:43-44

Matthew 24:45-51

Matthew 25:1-10

What is His main point in telling these stories?

IT'S ABOUT TIME

We are told throughout Revelation that "the time is at hand." Read the following passages. What did Jesus continually say about the Kingdom of God, and what are we to do in response?

Matthew 10:7

Mark 1:15

Luke 8:10

Chapter 2

THE COMING CHRIST

OVERVIEW

The full glory of Christ is revealed before John, and the prophet, overcome with awe, is told to write down what he sees. In this chapter, we will focus on ten attributes of Christ which John describes in this majestic vision.

INTRODUCTION • REVELATION 1:7-18

There are many descriptions of Christ throughout the Old and New Testaments, but none compares with the one provided by the Apostle John in Revelation 1:10-18. This is the first glimpse we have of the glorified Christ, the unveiled Son of God. As you go through this lesson, realize that you too will one day stand before Him in all His radiant splendor.

DISCUSSION

John's Situation

The Apostle John was given this vision while on the island of Patmos, off the western coast of Asia Minor. Patmos was the Alcatraz of that day, where people who had committed crimes against the state were sent. John had been banished there "for the word of God, and for the testimony of Jesus Christ" (Revelation 1:9).

To the believers of his time, John was indeed a "companion in tribulation"; the early church suffered terrible persecution under Roman rule. But this message is in no way less intended for today's church. We should be aware that the time is coming when believers—in all parts of the world—will once again experience persecution for the cause of Christ.

On the Lord's Day

"I was in the Spirit on the Lord's day, and heard behind me a great voice, as of a trumpet," writes John in Revelation 1:10. These are His instructions: "I am the Alpha and the Omega, the first and the last: What thou seest, write in a book, and send it unto the seven churches which are in Asia; unto Ephesus, and unto Smyrna, and unto Pergamos, and unto Thyatira, and unto Sardis, and unto Philadelphia, and unto Laodicea" (v. 11).

The Resurrected Christ

Not surprisingly, the first thing John does is to turn to see who is addressing him: "And I turned to see the voice that spake with me. And being turned, I saw seven golden candlesticks; and in the midst of the seven candlesticks one like unto the Son of man" (vv. 12-13).

Remember that it has been a full 60 years since John had last seen Jesus. But he immediately recognizes Him as "the Son of man." Jesus has not changed. He became a man at His birth in Bethlehem, He was resurrected as a man, He ascended to heaven as a man, and He will return as a man. Some people seem to believe that Jesus wore a "costume" of human flesh while He was on the earth and then discarded it when He went to heaven. But He is to keep His humanity for all eternity. And so John recognizes His Lord, the resurrected Christ—the Son of man.

The Reigning Christ

The next thing John notices about Jesus is His clothing. He was "clothed with a garment down to the foot, and girt about the paps [chest] with a golden girdle" (v. 13). These are not the kind of garments Jesus wore when He traveled through the hills of Galilee or when He walked the long journey to Jerusalem; these are the garments of a king. It is interesting to note that at Jesus' crucifixion, His clothes were taken from Him and divided by the casting of lots. He was covered in a purple robe, given a crown of thorns, and mocked (Matthew 27:27-31). The picture John gives us is very different. Jesus does not appear as the bloodied and beaten Savior, but as the King of Kings and the Lord of Lords.

The Righteous Christ

When John looks into Jesus' face, he sees that "his head and his hairs were white like wool, as white as snow" (v. 14). This symbolizes the purity and the righteousness of Christ. In Isaiah 1:18 God says, "Though your sins be as scarlet, they shall be as white as snow; though they be red like crimson, they shall be as wool." We are to understand that the whiteness of snow and the purity of bleached wool is symbolic of the purity of Christ. White, clean snow and soft wool seem like pleasant metaphors for purity; however, it is important to understand that the purity of Christ is of a nature that no one would be able to stand in His presence were it not for His mercy. The sinfulness of man cannot exist in the presence of the blinding holiness of Christ.

Christ is not pictured here as the advocate of sinners and the Savior of the world, but as the righteous Judge. And judge He will, for God has turned all judgment of sin over to Him.

The Revealing Christ

The second part of Revelation 1:14 says that Jesus' eyes "were as a flame of fire." He has vision that penetrates—or burns—to the core. Today we might say He has x-ray vision. He sees right through us. He knows about everything we've ever done. He knows about every thought we've ever had. He hears every lie and word of blasphemy that is uttered. Unlike any earthly judge, Jesus cannot be deceived. There was a story of a country man who was arrested for stealing a watch. At his trial, the prosecuting attorney did everything he could to prove the man's guilt, but there was not enough evidence. He could not be found guilty, so the judge told him, "Sam, you've been acquitted. You can go home." And the man replied, "Does that mean I have to give the watch back?"

Jesus cannot be deceived. He cannot be disbarred, disputed, or discredited. Not only does He see everything that happens, but He will reveal things that most people would like to keep hidden. There will be no more secrets or skeletons in closets when Jesus returns. He is the revealing Christ.

The Relentless Christ

In verse 15 we see that the feet of Jesus were "like unto fine brass, as if they burned in a furnace." In the Old Testament, brass is a symbol of judgment. In the temple that Solomon built, all of the instruments in the outer court were made of brass (1 Kings 7:40-47) because it was in the temple that sin was judged. Jesus' feet, which appear as burnished brass, are going forth to judge. He is unstoppable; there will be no escape from the wrath of God when Jesus' burning feet touch the earth. Christ will be relentless in His judgment of sin. At that time, those who have not allowed Him to deal with their sin on the cross will wish they had done so.

The Regal Christ

Until this point, John has tried to describe the appearance of Jesus. In the second part of verse 15, he says the sound of Jesus' voice is "as the sound of many waters." Imagine the sound of a roaring ocean or a waterfall crashing over the rocks far below.

Others have attributed the same qualities to the Lord's voice in Scripture. In Psalm 29:3-4, David writes: "The voice of the LORD is upon the waters: the God of glory thundereth...the voice of the Lord is full of majesty." The prophet Jeremiah was told: "Therefore prophesy thou against them all these words, and say unto them, the LORD shall roar from on high. A noise shall come even to the ends of earth; for the LORD hath a controversy with the nations" (Jeremiah 25:30-31).

Perhaps John had these Scriptures in mind when he tried to convey the majesty and earth-shaking power of the Lord's voice. The passage quoted above from Jeremiah says that the Lord's voice will be heard to the ends of the earth. It is easy to understand how, at the sight of Jesus with His eyes of blazing fire and His voice of thunder that "every knee should bow...and every tongue should confess that Jesus Christ is Lord" (Philippians 2:10-11). At Jesus' second coming, there will be no question as to His identity. Everyone—including His enemies—will acknowledge Him as King.

The Regulating Christ

Verse 16 begins: "And he had in his right hand seven stars..."

Frequently the symbolism of Revelation is self-explanatory, as is the case here. Jesus tells John in verse 20 that the seven stars represent the angels, or messengers, of the seven churches; the seven golden candlesticks represent the seven churches to whom John is to relay his vision.

Jesus holding the seven stars in His right hand signifies that He is the author and sustainer of all things—He is the regulator of the universe. Jesus is coming back to judge the world; He is also coming to setup and run His kingdom. The image of Jesus holding the seven stars reminds us that, no matter how chaotic and unstable the world becomes, He is ultimately in control of all things. No matter how the devil tries to destroy the church, it is under His protection. He will restore permanent order and harmony to His creation.

The Revenging Christ

Look again at verse 16: "Out of his mouth went a sharp two-edged sword."

The sharp, double-edged sword is, of course, the Word God, the Bible. In this instance it is not being used to instruct, correct, or edify, but to smite the nations in judgment (Revelation 2:16). Jesus is coming to take vengeance on His enemies. Those who have not submitted their lives to Christ through obedience to the Word will be struck down by it. Jesus refers to this in Matthew 10:34, but most likely, His disciples did not fully realize what He meant.

Jesus will be both judge and executioner. He will personally carry out the sentence handed down to the wicked. This is a disturbing thought for some people who do not like to think of Christ as one who seeks revenge. But he will not be acting out of hatred; He will be assuaging the righteous wrath of God towards those who have persistently violated His Word. They will have brought down its double-edged destruction upon themselves.

The Resplendent Christ

"His countenance was as the sun shineth in his strength (v. 16)." We've seen that Christ's clothes were like gold, His hair like snow, His feet like molten brass, and His eyes like fire; but most captivating of all is the light that radiates from His face. In the part of the world where John lived, the sunlight is usually very intense and unfiltered by clouds. You don't want to be exposed to it without a hat and sunglasses, and you certainly ought not to look anywhere near it. Such is the magnificent resplendence of Christ—as the brightest, noon-day sunlight.

The Apostle Paul was knocked from his horse when he saw the resplendence of Christ (Acts 9:3-9). It was three days before he regained his sight. Jesus' countenance is the light of heaven; our glorified bodies will be equipped with eyes that can bear to look upon the face of Jesus.

The Reassuring Christ

John's response to this vision of Christ is hardly surprising: He "fell at his feet as dead" (v. 17). But Jesus' intention is not to frighten John. "Fear not," He says, laying his hand upon the stunned Apostle. "I am the first and the last: I am he that liveth, and was dead; and, behold, I am alive for evermore, Amen; and have the keys of hell and of death."

Repeatedly, Scripture tells us that the day of the Lord's coming will be more awful than any the world has seen; and about the times leading up to it, Jesus said: "For then shall be great tribulation, such as was not since the beginning of the world to this time, no, nor ever shall be" (Matthew 24:21). And though believers will share in hardships and dreadful times, there can be no greater reassurance than that Christ has not only overcome the world, but sin and death also. We have nothing to fear from the coming judgment. Jesus our Lord is the one who is coming; He is the one who was dead but now lives forevermore.

APPLICATION

1. Read Revelation 1:7 again. Compare this description of Christ's arrival with His ascension into heaven in Acts 1:9-11. What promise did the angel give to the disciples? How does Zechariah 12:10 compare with Revelation 1:7? Why will Christ's return cause people to mourn?

2. Jesus repeats twice in Revelation 1:8 and in 1:11 that He is the "Alpha and the Omega." What do "Alpha and Omega" represent? Why might Jesus choose this way to describe Himself? Why not just "first and last"?

3. In what forms do you envision persecution taking place against the church in the Last Days? Can you see ways in which it is now taking place in your community?

4. How is Jesus' voice described in Revelation 1:10? In verse 15? Compare this with:

Isaiah 53:7

Matthew 27:12-14

Why do you think Jesus chose to remain silent at certain times?

5. Does there seem to be a conflict between the character of Jesus as we see Him in the Gospels and Jesus as He is pictured in Revelation 19:14-15? If so, consider that He is the "living Word of God;" what does Hebrews 4:12-13 say about the Word of God?

6. Read 2 Thessalonians 1:5-10. This was written to encourage the believers in Thessalonica. According to this, will God punish anyone unjustly? What fate awaits those who remain faithful to Him?

7. In the light of 2 Peter 3:9, is God anxious to "get on with the judgment"? Why or why not?

8. Consider the image of Christ holding the seven stars in His right hand (Revelation 1:16). How does this symbolize His supremacy? Read Colossians 1:15-20 and John 1:1-3. According to these passages, what was Christ's role in Creation? Is there any power or authority over which He does not have dominion?

9. From these passages, we can see how others have responded upon having an encounter with God:

   Luke 2:8-9

   Acts 9:3-9

   Exodus 33:18

   Do you feel that today's church has the same degree of reverence for God?

"I SAW THE LORD!"

There are several accounts in Scripture of people seeing the Lord. Note the similar responses in these four:

Isaiah 6:1-8

Luke 5:1-10

Acts 9

Revelation 1:9-18

Chapter 3

MAKING NUMBERS COUNT

OVERVIEW

In this lesson we will explore the symbolism and the signifiicance of numbers in Revelation.

INTRODUCTION • REVELATION 1:20

T he mystery of the seven stars which thou sawest in my right hand, and the seven golden candlesticks. The seven stars are the angels of the seven churches: and the seven candlesticks which thou sawest are the seven churches" (Revelation 1:20). Whether you understand that verse or not, you can see that the number seven is used many times.

DISCUSSION

Seven is a key number to understand the Revelation, a book that often uses numbers in a symbolic way. Chapters 1 through 4 tell of seven churches; chapters 4 through 7 speak of seven seals, and chapters 8 through 11 reveal seven trumpets You will also find seven persons in chapters 12 through 14, seven bowls in chapters 15 and 16, and seven judgments in chapters 17 through 20. You see, in Revelation, numbers count!

The Science of Numbers

God really wrote two books. He wrote this book we call the Bible, and He authored the book of nature. All of this world is like one great, big book that reveals God. Scripture tells us that nature speaks of God: "Day unto day uttereth speech, and night unto night sheweth knowledge" (Psalm 19:2). God speaks to us out of His book of nature.

You find numbers throughout nature, because God is a God of order. He is a God of design, a God of balance, and a God of mathematical precision. Astronomers studying the universe find that the heavens run according to mathematical law. They can make a chart and determine exactly where those heavenly bodies were thousands of years ago or precisely where they will be thousands of years into the future. The entire heavens run by mathematics.

The same is true of chemistry, zoology, and biology. They are all based upon mathematics. For example, there are trillions of cells in the human body. Each cell has forty-six chromosomes. Each animal has a set number of chromosomes that never varies. God is a Creator who built numbers into the universe. Numbers are a science created by God. Man didn't invent mathematical principles; he simply discovers them and learns how to use them.

The Symbolism of Numbers

To the authors of the Bible, numbers were more than a science. Numbers had a spiritual connotation, a deeper meaning. It is amazing how God uses numbers in a special way in Scripture—and it is just one more confirmation of the inspiration of Scripture. Each number has a special symbolism that the Lord uses in some unique way.

One

The number one is the number of unity and primacy; therefore, it speaks to us of God. Deuteronomy 6:4 says, "Hear O Israel, the

LORD our God is one LORD." Zechariah 14:9 tells us, "The LORD shall be king over all of the earth: in that day shall there be one Lord, and His name one." Paul teaches us in Ephesians 4:4-6 that "there is one body, and one Spirit, even as you are called in one hope of your calling; one Lord, one faith, one baptism, one God and Father of all, who is above all, and through all, and in you all."

"One" stands in the Bible for God, for primacy and unity that is summed up in the one great God. We don't worship three Gods; that would be polytheism. God has revealed Himself in three persons, but He is one God.

Two

Two in Scripture has the symbolic meaning of witness. For example, in John 8:17 we read, "It is also written in your law, that the testimony of two men is true." Two means that there will be witness and confirmation. We use that same idea at business meetings when one person makes a motion and another person says, "I second that motion." Even our Bible is divided into two sections, the Old and New Testaments. The Old Testament tells what is to come, and the New Testament confirms it.

Jesus is the second person of the Trinity, and in Revelation 1:5 He is called "the faithful witness." He sent His disciples out two by two so they could witness together. You will never improve on that way to witness either, because God's number of witness is two, and that is the meaning of the number.

Three

Three is a divine number. It speaks of the Holy Trinity. As one speaks of the unity of God, three speaks of His trinity. In Matthew 28:19 Jesus says to go ye therefore and teach all nations, baptizing them in the name of the Father, in the name of the Son, and in the name of the Holy Spirit—the three members of the Trinity. The one true God has revealed Himself to us in three Persons.

Man made in the image of God is triune in nature. He has body, soul, and spirit. First Thessalonians 5:23 says, "And I pray God your whole spirit and soul and body be preserved blameless unto the coming of our Lord Jesus Christ." Everything God has made reflects the tri-unity of Himself.

Four

Four stands for God's creation. Four is the number of the earth. "And he shall set up an ensign for the nations, and shall assemble the outcast of Israel, and gather together the dispersed of Judah from the four corners of the earth" (Isaiah 11:12). That is, God will gather His people from the four points of the compass, which represents the whole earth. In Ezekiel 7:2 we read, "Also thou son of man, thus saith the LORD GOD unto the land of Israel; an end, the end is come upon the four corners of the land." You see, four represents the earth. In Revelation 7:1 John writes, "After these things I saw four angels standing on the four corners of the earth, holding the four winds of the earth, that the wind should not blow on the earth, nor on the sea, nor on any tree." Even in heaven the number four is connected to creation, as there are four created beings around God's throne (Revelation 4:6). The number four is always linked to God's creation.

Multiples of these numbers retain similar meaning. For example, ten times four is forty, and forty has to do with earthly testing. Noah was in the ark while it rained for forty days and nights. Moses was on Mt. Sinai for forty days. The Jews wandered in the wilderness for forty years. Christ was tempted for forty days. The number four retains its meaning.

Five

The numbers five and ten are basically the same. They symbolize completeness. You have five senses, five fingers on each hand, five toes on each foot. If you lost a finger, you wouldn't be complete. So when God gave His complete moral law to Israel, He issued ten commandments.

It is interesting that in Revelation 13:1 the Antichrist is described with the number ten: "And I stood upon the sand of the sea, and saw a beast rise up out of the sea, having seven heads and ten horns." A horn in Bible prophecy was a symbol of power, so this beast with ten horns has complete power. This beast is going to completely rule the world in the last days. Notice also that on each horn there are ten crowns and upon his heads, the name of blasphemy. He will be totally blasphemous, a false king claiming to be God's representative.

Six

Six is the number of man. He was created on the sixth day. At the end of time, all men will be required to associate with the number six to buy or sell anything according to Revelation 13:18: "Let him that hath understanding count the number of the beast: for it is the number of a man; and his number is Six hundred threescore and six." The beast's number will be 666, and since three is the number of deity, the picture is of a man pretending to be God. And since seven is God's number, the number of perfection, man is just a six. Try as he may to be like God, all he amounts to is 666.

Seven

Do you know why seven is the number of perfection? It is a combination of the divine number three and the earth's number four. The earth is crowned with heaven. When God and earth get together, things start working out the way they are supposed to. Seven is the perfect number. So when John records, "These things saith he that hath the seven Spirits of God" (Revelation 3:1), he isn't saying that there are seven holy spirits, but that there is one perfect Holy Spirit. John is using the number seven symbolically. He does the same thing when He describes Jesus in chapter 5, verse 6: "In the midst of the throne and of the four beasts, and in the midst of the elders, stood a Lamb as it had been slain, having seven horns and seven eyes, which are the seven Spirits of God sent forth into all the earth." The Antichrist had complete power on earth, but Jesus has perfect power. The seven horns represent His perfect power, the seven eyes His perfect omniscience.

In chapters 2 and 3 of Revelation are messages to seven churches. These were actual churches, but the broader meaning is that these are messages for all churches. Each church has a lampstand, a seven-branched menorah that is the symbol of Israel even today. Each has six lower lights that represent man and one greater light in the middle that represents God. He alone can bring man to perfection. The church sends out the light of God's perfect message to lost man.

You will find sevens throughout Revelation because the book deals with God and heaven. The multiples of seven also refer to perfection, such as Christ's answer to Peter's question about forgiveness: "Seventy times seven." And note that seven cut in half spells disaster. Seven halved is three-and-one-half, and that invariably means the judgment of God. Elijah prayed for God to shut up the heavens, and it did not rain for three-and-one-half years. The Antichrist is going to make a covenant with Israel for seven years during the Great Tribulation, but he will break that agreement after three-and-one-half years. He will claim to be God and demand to be worshipped. Seven is the number of perfection, and the Antichrist will mimic perfection, but will actually be completely evil and corrupt.

Eight

The number eight speaks of new things. The eighth note on a piano begins a new octave, and the eighth day on the calendar begins a new week. Jewish babies were circumcised on the eighth day as a symbol of their salvation, their new life with God. Second Peter 2:5 reminds us that God "spared not the old world, but saved Noah the eighth person." Eight people were saved by God on the ark. Eight speaks of salvation, of new birth. Jesus rose from the dead on a Sunday, the eighth day, and He appeared to His disciples eight days later. Eight is the number of new beginnings.

Twelve

We have already talked about nine as a multiple of three and ten as a multiple of five, and I can find no symbolic significance to the number eleven, but twelve is God's governmental number. Just as seven is three plus four, twelve is three times four, the divine multiplied on the earth. That speaks of God's rule on earth, and the Lord always used the number twelve in setting up government. There were twelve patriarchs, twelve tribes of Israel, and twelve apostles in God's sovereignty. Matthew 19:28 reveals that at the end of time, "when the Son of man shall sit in the throne of his glory, ye also shall sit upon twelve thrones, judging the twelve tribes of Israel." The last few chapters of Revelation even describe the twelve gates of the holy city, which is 12,000 furlongs square, as the place where God's government is carried out. All of these numbers are used symbolically by God throughout the Revelation.

The Significance of Numbers

One tells us there is a God. Two that He has witnessed or spoken to you. Three that God exists as the Father, Son, and Holy Spirit. Four tells us that the worlds belongs to Him and is headed for His judgment. Five that He will finish what He started. Six tells us that we are sinners in need of salvation. Seven tells us of the perfect love God has for each of us. God demands perfection, but we cannot provide it, so eight tells us that we can be born again. He is the God who set everything into place, including all numbers and their meanings, and He wants each of us to turn to Him and be saved.

APPLICATION

1. How does science reveal God? If science reveals God, why do you think so much modern science seems to deny God's very existence? What does Paul have to say about God and science in Romans 1:18-32?

2. If one is God's symbolic number for unity, what do the following passages infer?

   Deuteronomy 6:4

   Zechariah 14:9

   Mark 12:32

   Ephesians 2:14-18

   Ephesians 4:3-6

3. In your own words, what does it mean that two stands for witness? What do the following verses reveal about the use of the number two:

Matthew 18:15-20

John 8:13-18

1 Timothy 5:19

Hebrews 10:28

How did Christ send out His witnesses in Luke 10:1-17?

How does the Lord bring the gospel message to a lost world in Revelation 11?

4. What does the number three symbolize? What evidences in Scripture are there to support your answer? What do Matthew 28:18-20 and 1 Thessalonians 5:23 teach us about the triune nature of God and man?

5. Why does the number four represent the earth? (See Isaiah 11:12, Ezekiel 37:9, and Daniel 11:4 for help.) Keeping in mind the symbolism of the number four, what significance do the four living creatures in Revelation 4:6-11 have?

6. Five and its multiple ten are the numbers of completeness. In what ways do we rely on ten? Where does the Lord use tens in Scripture?

7. If seven is the perfect number representing God, why is it significant that the number for man is six? What does Revelation 13:18 reveal about six? The word seven occurs 55 times in Revelation. What do you think is the significance of all those sevens (seven spirits, seven trumpets, seven bowls, etc.)?

8. What does the number eight symbolize? What principle do the following Old Testament law verses reveal about God's purposes for the number eight? (Exodus 22:30; Leviticus 9:1; 12:3; 14:10; 14:23; 15:14; 15:29; 22:27; 23:36, 39)

9. What significance do you find in the symbolic use of numbers in Scripture? What has been the most significant insight you have had while doing this study of numbers?

THE LORD IS ONE

The Jews used to memorize Deuteronomy 6:4-5 as the basic truth of their faith. Memorize these words: "Hear, O Israel: The LORD our God is one LORD. And thou shalt love the LORD thy God with all thine heart, and with all thy soul, and with all thy might."

Chapter 4

THE GOLDEN KEY
TO REVELATION

OVERVIEW

There is a three-fold outline to the Book of the Revelation that offers us a big-picture view of the end times.

INTRODUCTION • REVELATION 1:19

W rite the things which thou hast seen, and the things which are, and the things which shall be hereafter" (Revelation 1:19). That verse contains the golden key to the Book of the Revelation. This book, the last book of Scripture, is the counterpart to Genesis, the first book. In Genesis you see the creation of heaven and earth; in Revelation you see new heavens and a new earth. In Genesis you see paradise lost; in Revelation you see paradise regained. In Genesis you see man driven from the tree of life; in Revelation you see man invited back to that tree. In Genesis Satan appears for the first time; in Revelation he appears for the last time. In Genesis you see the beginning of sorrow, toil, pain, and death; in Revelation there is no more sorrow, nor crying, nor tears, for the old things are passed away. In Genesis you see the first Adam and his bride, Eve; in Revelation you see the last Adam

And His bride, the church of the Lord Jesus Christ. It is a thrilling book, and God wants to bless you through it.

DISCUSSION

John was commissioned by God to write the book and was told to write three things. As we examine those three things, we will get an overview of the end times.

The Things You Have Seen

John was first told to write the things he had seen. What had he seen? "I turned to see the voice that spake with me," John says in verse 12.

> *And being turned, I saw seven golden candlesticks; and in the midst of the seven candlesticks one like unto the Son of man, clothed with a garment down to the foot, and girt about the paps with a golden girdle. His head and his hairs were white like wool, as white as snow; and his eyes were as aflame of fire; and his feet like unto fine brass, as if they burned in a furnace; and his voice as the sound of many waters. And he had in his right hand seven stars: and out of his mouth went a sharp two-edged sword: and his countenance was as the sun shineth in his strength. And when I saw him, I fell at his feet as dead. And he laid his right hand upon me, saying unto me, Fear not; I am the first and the last: I am he that liveth and was dead; and, behold I am alive for evermore, Amen; and have the keys of hell and death. Write the things which thou hast seen.* (Revelation 1:12-19)

The first division in God's outline of the book is a vision of the Lord Jesus Christ. John saw Jesus. He didn't see Him primarily as Savior, but as Sovereign. He didn't see Jesus as Justifier, but as Judge. He didn't see Christ in His humiliation, but in His glorification. John had a vision of the crucified, risen, ascended, glorified, and coming Christ. And that is what the Book of Revelation is written to present: an unveiling of Jesus Christ in all His glory, all His majesty, as He comes to reign as King of kings and Lord of lords.

Some people ask, "Why didn't Jesus appear this way the first time He came? Why did He come meekly, wandering the shores of Galilee?" The answer is because He wants you to choose to follow Him. Had He come in power and might the first time, you would have been afraid not to follow Him. When Jesus was on earth people were always asking Him to do miracles as a sign of His deity. But Christ couldn't be taunted into miracles. He often warned people not to tell of His miracles because He wasn't doing them as publicity stunts. He wants men to love Him for who He is, not what He can do. He wants men and women to turn to Him because of His beauty and nature, not just His power and might. So He laid aside all the splendor and glory that was inherently His, left His throne, and was born of a virgin in a barn, raised in obscurity. He came as a nondescript person; Isaiah even says there is no form, nor comeliness, nor beauty that we should desire Him. Yet all the nature of God was in the Lord Jesus Christ, and that causes a right heart to respond to Him by faith. Just as healthy eyes respond naturally to light, your heart responds naturally to Christ.

If He had come in a dazzling display of glory the first time, some would have followed Him because of what He could do. Even if He came today in all His glory, people everywhere would fall on their faces before Him overwhelmed—but not necessarily saved. So He came in His humanity the first time to redeem us. And his friend, John, exiled to the island of Patmos for preaching the Gospel, was told to write about seeing Jesus.

The Things Which Are

The second part of John's message was to write about the things which are, which is to say, the present age. Chapters 2 and 3 are messages to seven churches that describe this church age. They give insight into the present age. As we have already seen, these seven churches were actual churches in Asia minor, but they symbolically represent all churches. As a matter of fact, a quick reading of those chapters reveals the word *church* popping up over and over again. These chapters describe the church in the church age, which began with the apostles and goes right through to the rapture. We are living in the period of time known as the things which are, the church age. And there is not a church problem left untouched by those seven messages to the seven churches.

It starts with the church at Ephesus, with the Lord saying they have left their first love. He doesn't say that they don't love the Lord, only that they don't love Him like they used to. He has a message for each of the churches, though that is another study all on its own. Christ tells the church at Smyrna to stand firm in the face of tribulation, and He warns the church at Pergamos not to allow false teachers. He criticizes the church at Thyatira for not dealing with sin in its body, urges the dead church at Sardis to turn back to Him, and encourages the weak church at Philadelphia to become strong in the faith. Finally, the Lord tells the lukewarm church at Laodicea, "Because thou sayest, I am rich, and increased with goods, and have need of nothing; and knowest not that thou art wretched, and miserable, and poor, and blind, and naked" (Revelation 3:17). These people had become indifferent to God, saying, "I love you, but I'm not excited about you." That is blasphemy! We ought to stay in love with the Lord Jesus Christ.

The message to those churches is that we must be careful each day to keep a passionate, burning love for God alive in our hearts. If you don't love Him like that, you'll experience all kinds of problems. If you want your church to remain strong and healthy, if you want to remain godly and pure, stay in love with Jesus Christ. That's the principle behind the church messages in chapters 2 and 3.

The Things Which Shall Be

The third division in the Book of the Revelation is by far the largest. Chapters 4 through 22 comprise this third section, which focuses on prophecy. John was told to write the things he had seen, then the things which are, and now he writes about the things which shall be in the future. The Lord Jesus Christ is coming back to rule and reign here on earth. John offers us an outline of the broad panorama of church history. Too many times people will read about single events of the end times—Armageddon, or the Millennium, or the Antichrist—and the story becomes confused because they don't see the big picture. Starting in chapter 4, John offers the reader the big picture of the last days.

"After this I looked, and, behold, a door was opened in heaven: and the first voice which I heard was as it were of a trumpet talking with me; which said, Come up hither, and I will show thee things which must be hereafter" (Revelation 4:1). Those words *after this* literally mean "after these things," so I believe that means "after the church age." When John was caught up to the throne of God, that is a picture of all believers being caught up to the throne at the Rapture. First Corinthians 15:52 and 1 Thessalonians 4:16 both tell us there is going to be a trumpet blown when the Lord comes, and John describes a voice that sounds like a trumpet. God is going to call His children to Himself, and we will all be drawn immediately up to heaven to meet the Lord in the air. That's the Rapture, when Christians will be caught up to be with God, the very first event in God's prophetic calendar.

The next event, which takes place immediately after the Rapture, is the Great Tribulation. This will be a period of seven years when Satan really runs things on earth. Revelation 9:6 epitomizes this time period: "And in those days shall men seek death, and shall not find it; and shall desire to die, and death shall flee from them." The world will be infested with demonic spirits who will inflict torture upon men, and mankind, whose first instinct is self-preservation, will prefer death to life. That exemplifies how terrible the Great Tribulation will be.

That seven-year period will end with the Battle of Armageddon. The Antichrist will have become a virtual world dictator, holding sway over the earth. He will make a treaty with Israel for seven years, and Israel will think she is safe. But after three and one-half years, he will break that treaty, set himself up in the rebuilt temple, and demand Israel's worship. The Jewish people, who mistook the Antichrist for the Messiah, will realize they have been betrayed and refuse to worship him. So he will turn on them with satanic fury and seek to destroy Israel. He will call all the armies to the plain of Armageddon to make war with Israel. That battle will be interrupted by the return of Jesus Christ, riding a white horse, with the saints dressed in white linen behind Him.

And I saw the beast, and the kings of the earth, and their armies, gathered together to make war against him that sat on the horse, and against his army. And the beast was taken, and with him the false prophet that wrought miracles before him, with which he deceived them that had received the mark of the beast, and them that worshiped his image. These both were cast alive into a lake of fire burning with brimstone (Revelation 19:19-20).

At that time the Jews will look to the Lord Jesus Christ. They will see Him for who He is, and they will weep that they rejected their long-awaited Messiah when He walked the earth. They will believe in Him, and He will reign on earth for a thousand years. This is the Millennium, when Christ sets up His kingdom on earth. Some people believe that when Christ comes back, God is done with His plan for the earth. But God has made a promise that Jesus will rule from the throne of His father David. Jesus will literally, bodily, rule from Jerusalem.

The next event is the final judgment of the unsaved dead. And I saw a great white throne, and him that sat on it, from whose face the earth and the heaven fled away; and there was found no place for them. And I saw the dead, small and great, stand before God; and the books were opened: and another book was opened, which is the book of life: and the dead were judged out of those things which were written in the books, according to their works. And the sea gave up the dead which were in it; and death and hell delivered up the dead which were in them: and they were judged every man according to their works. And death and hell were cast into the lake of fire. This is the second death. And whosoever was not found written in the book of life was cast into the lake of fire (Revelation 20:11-15).

The final judgment doesn't occur until the end of time, so a man's actions and the repercussions of his actions can fully be judged.

Finally, the last two chapters of Revelation describe the new heaven and the new earth that God creates. They are beautiful chapters that tell of what God has in store for His people: "And God shall wipe away all tears from their eyes, and there shall be no more death, neither sorrow, nor crying, neither shall there be any more pain: for the former things are passed away...and there shall be no night there; and they need no candle, neither light of the sun; for the Lord God giveth them light: and they shall reign for ever and ever" (Revelation 21:4; 22:5).

APPLICATION

1. In Revelation 1:19, John was told to first write "the things he had seen." What had he seen? How does he describe Jesus Christ?

2. Why didn't Christ come in power and glory the first time He visited earth?

3. John next was told to write of "the things that are." In your own words, sum up Christ's message to the seven churches of Asia. How does this message apply to the church today?

4. The third thing John was told to write was "things which shall be." Why do you suppose God wants us to know what will happen in the end times?

5. What do the following passages reveal about the end times?

    Matthew 24:30-31

    Matthew 25:31-33, 46

    Luke 21:7-33

    1 Corinthians 15:51-57

IT'S ABOUT TIME

On a separate sheet of paper create a timeline by writing the events of the end times, along with the time each will take place.

Chapter 5

A GLIMPSE INTO GLORY

OVERVIEW

John was invited to catch a glimpse at the marvelous plan of God for the ages. In this study we will begin exploring what he observed in the presence of God.

INTRODUCTION • REVELATION 4

Many people think of eternity as being "way out there." But eternity is just around the corner, a heartbeat away. In the twinkling of an eye we can be in eternity. The things that take place in the Revelation happen quickly, and we have already seen incredibly quick changes in our world.

In our lifetimes alone, we have seen the development of atomic weapons, space exploration, worldwide communication, the remarkable advancement of computers, and the restoration of the nation of Israel. In May of 1948 the Republic of Israel was born, and that area of the planet immediately became the focal point of the world politically, militarily, and economically. We have suddenly been able to understand how the world could be destroyed with nuclear weapons, how the entire world can watch events unfolding live on television, and how computers can turn us into a cashless society, controlling our lives to the point where we won't be able to buy or sell without receiving a computer access code number. Many Christians have the feeling that there is something in the air, that the world is fast approaching a time when our Lord and Savior Jesus Christ will burst through the clouds to the sound of trumpets and take His children home with Him.

DISCUSSION

After this I looked, and, behold, a door was opened in heaven: and the first voice which I heard was as it were of a trumpet talking with me; which said, Come up hither, and I will show thee things which must be hereafter. And immediately I was in the Spirit: and, behold, a throne was set in heaven, and one sat on the throne.
(Revelation 4:1-2)

Notice that John begins with the words after these things, in other words, after the church age. We live in the church age, and after this age these things John writes about will happen.

The Rapture

John's attention is suddenly turned heavenward to a voice like a trumpet. A door opens, John hears a call, and then he is caught up to heaven. These events speak of the Rapture. First Thessalonians 4:15-17 describes the Rapture this way:

We which are alive and remain unto the coming of the Lord shall not prevent them which are asleep. For the Lord Himself shall descend from heaven with a shout, with the voice of the archangel, and with the trump of God: and the dead in Christ shall rise first: then we which are alive and remain shall be caught up together with them in the clouds, to meet the Lord in the air: and so shall we ever be with the Lord.

Why is the Lord calling the church up? Because He is about to pour His wrath out upon the earth. The Great Tribulation is about to commence, so before it begins the church must be taken out. I do not believe the church will go through the Tribulation period. God is not going to pour out His wrath upon His own dear children. He will chastise us when we stray from Him, but He will never pour out His wrath on us. God has not appointed us to wrath, but to obtain salvation through our Lord Jesus Christ.

There is a pattern in Scripture that, before God metes out judgment, He takes out His own. For example, in Matthew 24:38-39 Jesus says, "For as in the days that were before the flood, they were eating and drinking, marrying and giving in marriage, until the day that Noah entered into the ark, and knew not until the flood came, and took them all away." During that evil time, before God sent His judgment upon wicked mankind, He protected His people on the ark. The world was going about its business, and suddenly the Lord came. In the Great Tribulation, people will not be eating and drinking and marrying; they will be infested with demons, praying for death in the midst of the hell that is earth. "So shall also the coming of the Son of man be," Christ continues. "Then shall two be in the field; the one shall be taken, the other left. Two women shall be grinding at the mill; the one shall be taken, and the other left. Watch therefore; for ye know not what hour your Lord doth come" (Matthew 24:40-41).

Watching for the Lord

Christians are always to be watching for the Lord, not just waiting for the Tribulation. His return is imminent and will take place at the end of this church age. We don't know when it will be, but it will be soon. One of the reasons I don't believe the church will go through the Tribulation is because then we would know exactly when Christ would return and set up His kingdom. He will come first to take the Christians out of this world, and we are to be ready for Him. There won't be any time to say, "God, have mercy! I've decided to change my life!" There won't be any time to become a soul-winner or a tither or make amends to those we have hurt. He will just come, and we had best be ready.

Behold the Throne

The first thing John saw was a throne. Won't it be wonderful to behold His throne? To see Christ on the throne of glory? There are three things I want you to see: the person upon the throne, the people before the throne, and the praise unto the throne.

The Person Upon the Throne

Look at how the text describes the person on the throne: "He that sat was to look upon like a jasper and a sardine stone: and there was a rainbow round about the throne, in sight like unto an emerald" (Revelation 4:3). This passage describes His glory. "Jasper" is not the opaque stone of today. As described in Revelation 21:11, it is clear as crystal. I think this is what today we call a diamond. John looks at the one sitting on the throne and sees His radiance, His brilliance, His purity, like a beautiful diamond. It is an incredibly beautiful sight. Notice that there is also a "sardine stone," which is blood red, symbolic of the sacrifice of Christ. The one seated on the throne is infinitely loving, and He shed His blood on the cross for you and me.

The high priest of Old Testament days wore a breastplate that held twelve stones, one jewel for each of the twelve tribes of Israel. It was a symbol for the fact that God has His people upon His heart, and the first and last stone of that breastplate were jasper and sardine stone. So this portrayal of Jesus in Revelation 4 speaks of His love and oneness with His people. He is great in glory, and He is great in grace.

The Rainbow

"And there was a rainbow round about the throne, in sight like unto an emerald." Perhaps you've seen a circular rainbow from way up in an airplane, but no one in John's day had ever been high enough to see anything like that. He describes the rainbow in a circle, a perfect geometric figure that symbolizes eternity—no beginning and no end. It is green like an emerald, which is the color of life. In other words, the rainbow signifies eternal life, and it is the same symbol God hung in the sky after the flood to remind people of His covenant promise. The emerald rainbow around that throne speaks of a God who will keep His promises.

Of course, a rainbow signifies that the storm is over. At this future time the storm will be over for all Christians. The great and gracious God will be faithful to show mercy to His children.

Great in Government

Notice in verse 5 that "out of the throne proceeded lightnings and thunderings and voices: and there were seven lamps of fire burning before the throne, which are the seven Spirits of God." The thunder, lightnings, and voices seem to build to a crescendo. They tell us that, even though the storm is over for the child of God, another is about to break loose upon the earth. There is impending judgment in the lightning and thunder, and God's great government is about to work itself out on earth. The first thing John sees is one upon the throne who is great in glory, great in grace, and great in government.

The People Before the Throne

"And round about the throne there were four and twenty seats: and upon the seats I saw four and twenty elders sitting, clothed in white raiment; and they had on their heads crowns of gold" (v. 4). The word translated *seats* is also translated *thrones*, so you will find twenty-four men on thrones in the presence of God! These are not angels, since they are seated on thrones, wearing crowns, and, according to Revelation 5:8, singing—activities never ascribed to angels in Scripture. These people are wearing white raiment, symbolic of having been cleansed. They are wearing crowns, so they are co-heirs with Christ. These are the redeemed, the saints. These are the ones caught up to heaven at the Rapture. They symbolize all the saints of all the ages. John saw the people of God around the throne, wearing the "crown of righteousness" that Paul speaks of in 2 Timothy 4:8.

The twenty-four elders are symbolic numbers for God's people, caught up in glory. Jesus "loved us, and washed us from our sins in his own blood, and hath made us kings and priests unto God and his Father; to Him be glory and dominion for ever and ever. Amen" (Revelation 1:5-6). That will be you and me around God's throne. Cleansed by the blood of Jesus, given a crown of righteousness, and praising God for all eternity.

Praise Unto the Throne

The worship of God was first set up in the temple, which had an order and precision to it. There was the ark, the lampstand, and the other articles, each of which represented something about God and His relationship to us. That pattern will be repeated in heaven.

The Lamp

"And there were seven lamps of fire burning before the throne, which are the seven Spirits of God" (Revelation 4:5). This does not mean there are seven Holy Spirits, but that the perfect number seven symbolizes the perfect Holy Spirit. And the Spirit is like a perfect seven-pronged lamp, representing the perfect worship of God. There was a seven-pronged lampstand in front of the Ark of the Covenant in the original temple. Its job was to cast light on the Ark. The Holy Spirit's role is to cast light on Jesus Christ in our lives so that we can see Him and understand Him better.

The Sea of Glass

"And before the throne there was a sea of glass like unto crystal" (v. 6). Remember that in the temple was a large basin filled with water—called a sea—that the priest would use to wash himself. In one sense, that sea represented the Word of God, which cleanses us. Around the throne of God there will be another sea, this one filled with glass, pure and clear. It still stands for the Word of God, but no longer do we wash in it. There is no need to, for we are made like Christ. Now we can stand on that Word, for it is firm. What a beautiful picture: We stand upon the Word of God and are cleansed, and that Word is so solid in heaven it becomes our foundation. We won't have to wash anymore; we have been cleansed for all time, and we stand on that promise.

The Beasts

> In the midst of the throne, and round about the throne, were four beasts full of eyes before and behind. And the first beast was like a lion, and the second beast like a calf, and the third beast had a face as a man, and the fourth beast was like a flying eagle. And the four beasts had each of them six wings about him; and they were full of eyes within: and they rest not day and night, saying, Holy, holy, holy, Lord God Almighty, which was, and is, and is to come. (Revelation 4:6-8)

These aren't beasts like those associated with the Antichrist. Another word that can be translated *creatures* is used here. There are four creatures of God, and you will remember that the number four represents creation. So this is a depiction of all created things worshiping God. God made a covenant with all living things after the flood that He would redeem all things, and someday He will.

The reason He created all things was to bring glory to Himself. That is why everyone shouts to God, "Thou art worthy, O Lord, to receive glory and honor and power: for thou hast created all things, and for thy pleasure they are and were created" (Revelation 4:11). All creation will bow down to worship Him, and when they do the saints, too, will "fall down before Him...and cast their crowns before the throne" (v. 10). Some day all believers will look at their Savior and say, "Lord, this crown is not mine to wear. I cast it at your feet and give you all glory and honor forever."

These things can all happen at any time. Where will you be? Casting your crown before the Lord God, or preparing for the Great Tribulation?

APPLICATION

1. How does Revelation 4:1 imply the rapture of the church?

2. What principles for worship do you glean from the following passages from the Psalms:

   Psalm 5:7

   Psalm 22:27-31

Psalm 29:1-2

Psalm 66:1-4

Psalm 86:9-10

Psalm 95:1-7

Psalm 97:1-10

Psalm 99:4-5

3. How would you describe a true worship experience? What attitude must we have to worship God? What actions are necessary for worship?

4. What attitude does Paul display in Ephesians 3:14-21, and how can we imitate it?

5. What was the most dynamic worship experience you ever had? What made it so emotional?

6. On a scale of 1 to 100, how ready are you to meet Jesus at the Rapture? Read 1 John 2:28. What needs to happen for you to meet Jesus confident and unashamed?

SEEING CHRIST IN ME

Philippians 2:5-11 was originally an early church hymn. Memorize that passage or try setting it to music.

Chapter 6

WORTHY IS THE LAMB

OVERVIEW

In Revelation 5 we find John fascinated with a book in the hand of God. That book offers a fascinating insight into the relationship of Christ and the world.

INTRODUCTION • REVELATION 5

"And I saw in the right hand of him that sat on the throne a book written within and on the backside, sealed with seven seals" (Revelation 5:1). John's attention is caught by a book, literally a scroll, in the right hand of the Almighty as He sits on His throne in heaven. Notice that the book is "written within," that is, the words are written on a long piece of paper and then the paper is rolled up onto itself so that the words are concealed. The Romans were known for writing one important piece of information, then rolling the paper and sealing it with wax and an official seal. Then more words would be written, the paper would be rolled some more, and another seal would be added. Often a king would send important state documents with a series of seals on them. The outer seal would warn the person holding the scroll that no one was to break the seal unless they were qualified to possess the information contained within. This particular book had seven seals.

DISCUSSION

This scroll, which some find so mysterious, is the title deed to the earth. It is the official document that will determine the outcome of human history. Bearing in mind that much of the symbolism of Revelation must be interpreted in light of the Old Testament, take a look at Jeremiah 32. The prophet Jeremiah was warned by God that Israel would be captured by the Babylonians, and the people would be in captivity for seventy years. But God also tells the prophet to purchase a piece of land in Israel as a symbolic act that, someday, they will retake possession of their land. So Jeremiah buys a plot of land from his cousin Hanameel for seventeen shekels of silver, "and I subscribed the evidence, and sealed it, and took witnesses, and weighed him the money in the balances" (Jeremiah 32:10). That is to say, Jeremiah wrote an agreement, then got witnesses, then sealed it so there could be no tampering with it. There were actually two parts to this written agreement. One was given to a witness as a matter of public record, and the other was stored in a clay jar for safe keeping. That is the method God's people had for documenting purchases, and it is illustrative for the scroll in Revelation 5.

The book in the hand of God is a document redeeming the world. It is a sealed scroll, a legal document, belonging to the One who has paid the price and therefore has the legal right to open it and reveal what is written within. It is the title deed to the earth.

The Tragic Weakness of Civilization

"And I saw a strong angel proclaiming with a loud voice, Who is worthy to open the book, and to loose the seals thereof? And no man in heaven, nor in earth, neither under the earth, was able to open the book, neither to look thereon. And I wept much, because no man was found worthy to open and to read the book, neither to look thereon" (Revelation 5:2-4).

A challenge is thrown out to all humanity: Who has the right to the title deed to the earth? Who has paid the price to redeem it and can legally open those seals? No one answers. There is no one on earth, in heaven, or in hell who is worthy of opening it. No pastor, no politician, no philosopher or scientist. God reveals the weakness of human civilization in this one act. No one is able to save this sin-cursed world.

It is important to notice that the angel does not ask who is willing, but rather who is worthy. Alexander the Great was willing to rule the earth. Napoleon was willing, as were Genghis Kahn, Caesar, and Adolph Hitler. But none was worthy. Even Abraham, Moses, and David were unworthy, unable to take this book, redeem the world, and reign on earth. And John sobs openly, because he knows that this world needs redemption. The world needs a leader, and the scroll must be opened and the seals broken for God's purposes to be fulfilled. Without someone worthy of opening that scroll, John realizes that his life has been in vain. He has been exiled for no reason, and his friends martyred for a lost cause. There would be no hope for Israel, no peace in the world, no saving from sin and destruction. So his heart is broken and he weeps over the tragic weakness of civilization.

The Triumphant Worthiness of Christ

> *And one of the elders saith unto me, Weep not: behold, the Lion of the tribe of Judah, the Root of David, hath prevailed to open the book, and to loose the seven seals thereof. And I beheld, and lo, in the midst of the throne and of the four beasts, and in the midst of the elders, stood a Lamb as it had been slain, having seven horns and seven eyes, which are the seven Spirits of God sent forth into all the earth. And he came and took the book out of the right hand of him that sat upon the throne.* (Revelation 5:5-7)

John is told not to cry; there is good news! Someone has been found who can open that scroll and read it. Someone is worthy and has paid the price to redeem the world.

The Power of Our Lord

Jesus is described as the Lion of the tribe of Judah. The lion is the king of beasts. He has regal power. The Jews were looking for a lion-like Messiah to cast off the yoke of Rome. They were looking for one who would reign in splendor and might, who would restore the majesty to Israel. But when Jesus came, with His simplicity, meekness, and teaching about turning the other cheek, they rejected Him. He was an all-powerful lion, but He came to them as a lamb.

So in heaven, John turns to look at the Lion of the tribe of Judah, and what does he see? There in their midst stands a lamb. And the Greek word John uses means a pet lamb—a little, cuddly, baby lamb. John turns, looking for the mighty, ferocious lion, and finds a tender lamb as it had been slain. And that reveals the power of God. You see, Satan is described as a dragon, with his hordes of mighty demons supporting him in his evil work. But God is so powerful that all He requires to defeat Satan is a little pet lamb.

Notice that the Lamb is standing, even though it had been slain. How can that be? Jesus was killed, but He conquered death and is now alive. The Lamb is slain, but the Lamb is standing. And the Lamb is strong. He has seven horns, and the horn is the Jewish symbol of power. Seven, God's perfect number, means that Christ has perfect power. And He has seven eyes, which is symbolic language to mean He sees everything. He is the searching Lamb. He has perfect knowledge. Paul, in 1 Corinthians 1:24, calls Christ "the power of God, and the wisdom of God"—seven horns and seven eyes.

We look for Christ as a lion, but He is revealed in Scripture as something very different. In the words of John the Baptist, He is "the lamb of God who takes away the sin of the world."

The Position of Our Lord

Notice where Christ is in Revelation 5:6: "And I beheld, and, lo, in the midst of the throne and of the four beasts, and in the midst of the elders, stood a Lamb." Christ is right there in the middle of everyone. Perhaps John did not notice Him at first because he was struck by the beauty of the rainbow or he was amazed at the story of the scroll, but somehow John failed to recognize Jesus. That can happen to us. Some people get so wrapped up in their religion that they actually miss ever meeting Jesus. It is possible to do a study like this one and get so caught up in prophecy that you fail to see whom the prophecies glorify. In the middle of all these events is the Lamb of God. Keep that in mind as you study your Bible. Jesus is central to everything in the Book of Revelation.

The Prerogatives of Our Lord

The Lamb came "and took the book out of the right hand of him that sat upon the throne (v. 7)." By what prerogative does

He do this? Because He is worthy. Why has He been judged worthy to rule and reign? There are several reasons. First, He is worthy because He created all things. Take a look back at 4:11, which says, "Thou art worthy, O Lord, to receive glory and honour and power: for thou hast created all things, and for thy pleasure they are and were created." The universe was created by Him and for Him. He made everything, so he has a right to rule over His creation.

Second, He is worthy by the right of conquest. As the elder says in verse 5, "The Root of David hath prevailed." He has conquered Satan. He has conquered sin. He has conquered death. He has conquered the world, and by the right of conquest, the Lamb has this prerogative.

Third, He is worthy to take possession of this world because of Calvary. Verse 9 reads, "Thou art worthy to take the book, and open the seals thereof: for thou wast slain, and hast redeemed us to God by thy blood." Because He suffered and died on a cross in our place, He is worthy to open the scroll, worthy to rule and reign on earth.

The Thrilling Worship of Creation

And I beheld, and I heard the voice of many angles round about the throne, and the beasts, and the elders: and the number of them was ten thousand times ten thousand, and thousands of thousands; saying with a loud voice, Worthy is the Lamb that was slain to receive power, and riches, and wisdom, and strength, and honor, and glory, and blessing. And every creature which is in heaven, and on earth, and under the earth, and such as are in the sea, and all that are in them, heard I saying, Blessing, and honor and glory, and power, be unto him that sitteth upon the throne, and unto the Lamb forever and ever. And the four beasts said, Amen. And the four and twenty elders fell down and worshiped him that liveth forever and ever. (Revelation 5:11-14)

If Jesus is not God, He is not to be worshipped. John reveals that the Lamb is being worshipped in heaven. Modern scholars and philosophers will try to tell you that Jesus was not God. They will tip their hats to Him as a good man, but they will not bow their knees to Him as Almighty God. But He is worthy to be worshipped. The theme of all creation is that He is worthy to be worshipped. Someday everyone on earth, in heaven, and in hell will acknowledge

Christ and give Him glory. His sacrifice will be praised forever and ever. There are some denominations who have gone through their hymnals and taken out all the songs about the blood of Jesus. But the whole purpose of worshipping Him is because of His blood. The reason He is worthy is because of the cross at Calvary. You will see as you get further into Revelation that Christ's precious blood is the theme of all the saints through all the ages. They are worshipping Him in praise, and they sing about His blood shed on the cross that redeems them. Even if there were no heaven and hell, which there are, I would live my life for Jesus Christ for He is worthy. And if I had 1,000 lives to live, I would give every one of them to Christ. With my soul, with everything that is within me, I want to give glory to Him. He is worthy and will be worshipped by everyone throughout all eternity.

APPLICATION

1. According to Exodus 20:1-11, in what ways are we called to worship God? What is the significance in the order of those commandments? Restate verse 3 in your own words.

2. How did worship change with the death of Jesus Christ? (Hebrews 4:14-16; 7:27-28; 9:1-28; 10:1-4, 9-12)

3. How does worship change us and help us grow?

4. According to Psalm 27:4, what did David say was his focus? What does Paul say in Philippians 3:10? What is Jude's prayer in Jude 24-25? Look at the focus of John's life in 1 John 1:1-4. What is the common theme in the lives of all these men?

5. What would you say is the focus of your church? What is the one-word focus of your life?

THE PSALMS OF LIFE

Many of the Psalms tell the story of God's mighty power. Write your own Psalm or poem about the great things God has done in your life.

Chapter 7

THE FOUR HORSEMEN OF THE APOCALYPSE

OVERVIEW

In this study we will open the first six seals of the scroll and discover the future events of the world.

INTRODUCTION • REVELATION 6

Many people have heard of the four horsemen of the apocalypse, but few know what they represent. They are associated with a terrible time in history, as Revelation 6:15-17 makes clear:

> *And the kings of the earth, and the great men, and the rich men, and the chief captains, and the mighty men, and every bondman, and every free man, hid themselves in the dens and in the rocks of*

the mountains; and said to the mountains and rocks, Fall on us,
and hide us from the face of him that sitteth on the throne, and
from the wrath of the Lamb. For the great day of his wrath is
come; and who shall be able to stand?

These verses speak of the Great Tribulation Period, an awful time for this world. The Lord Jesus had this to say about that time: "For then shall be great tribulation, such as was not since the beginning of the world to this time, no, nor ever shall be" (Matthew 24:21). That is a remarkable statement. Considering all the wars, all the famines, all the heartache and sickness and atrocities that have taken place on earth, to hear Jesus say there is a bad time coming, the likes of which the earth has never seen, makes one tremble. Jesus went on to say that those days will be so devastating, God will bring them to a merciful premature conclusion, or there would be no one left alive on the earth.

The Prophet Jeremiah likewise warns of this time. "Wherefore do I see every man with his hands on his loins, as a woman in travail, and all faces turned to paleness? Alas! For that day is great, so that none is like it: it is even the time of Jacob's trouble" (Jeremiah 30:6-7). A time is coming when men will go around with their hands wrapped around their loins like women giving birth, their faces ashen at the terrible things happening on earth. And the whole world will be focused on Israel.

In Daniel 12:1 the prophet says, "And there shall be a time of trouble, such as never was since there was a nation even to that same time: and at that time thy people shall be delivered, every one that shall be found written in the book." The Jews will be delivered out of the Great Tribulation, but their deliverance will be at the very end of time.

DISCUSSION

John, in a vision of heaven, has seen a scroll given to the Lord Jesus Christ. It is the deed to the earth, and Jesus is the only one worthy of opening it and finding out what will happen to the world. As the scroll is unrolled, one at a time the seals are broken and the judgments of God are unveiled.

The First Seal: Dominion

"And I saw when the Lamb opened one of the seals, and I heard, as it were the noise of thunder, one of the four beasts saying, Come and see" (Revelation 6:1). The noise of thunder is at hand because the storm is about to break over the earth. John sees one of the four beasts, which represent the created beings of God, speaking. The translation "Come and see," is not really clear. Those words are better translated, "Go see" or "Ride forth." Rather than an invitation for John to see what is happening, it is a message to the first horse and rider that it is time for them to get to work. "And I looked, and behold a white horse: and he that sat on him had a bow; and a crown was given unto him: and he went forth conquering, and to conquer" (v. 2).

Remember that when this scene takes place, the church has already been raptured out of the world. The church is gone. And a rider on a white horse goes forth. In the Bible, a white horse symbolizes conquest. When an ancient king would come back victorious from the battlefield, he would ride a white charger. So here is the Antichrist riding forth to conquer the world. He has a crown on, so he is some sort of king, and he is holding a bow as a symbol of power and warfare. The Antichrist rides forth upon his white horse, seeming to be an invincible conqueror. However, note that the crown was given to him. It is the sovereign God who has allowed this evil man to come to power. In fact, God will cause it to come to pass so that He can accomplish His purposes: "For God hath put in their hearts to fulfill his will, and to agree, and give their kingdom unto the beast, until the words of God shall be fulfilled" (Revelation 17:17). God will convince the kings and rulers of the world to give up their power to the Antichrist. Satan will think he has won a victory, but it is all in God's plan.

There is a ten-nation confederacy right now in Europe called the Common Market, and I believe that, sooner or later, they are going to join together and surrender power to one world leader. He is going to be given a crown. It is not something he deserves, but it is something God Almighty will allow because He plans to give mankind enough rope to hang himself. So this first rider goes forth with military power and a political crown, to conquer and gain dominion.

Jesus is coming at the end of Revelation on a white horse also. But His coming will be very different from this false Christ.

He will be wearing a true crown, a diadem. And He will have a sword coming out of His mouth, which is to say, He will speak the truth of the ages. And He will come to rule and reign in all power and in peace. That second coming is contrasted to this false Christ's coming at the start of the Tribulation.

The Second Seal: Division

"And when he had opened the second seal, I heard the second beast say, Come and see. And there went out another horse that was red; and power was given to him that sat thereon to take peace from the earth, and that they should kill one another; and there was given unto him a great sword" (vv. 3-4). It is a fact of history that when a devil-inspired leader comes upon the world stage with ideas of conquest in his evil mind, there always follows war and havoc and destruction. This second rider appears on a red horse, the symbol of war because it is the color of blood.

General Omar Bradley once said about our generation, "We know more about war than about peace. We know more about killing than about living. This is our twentieth century's claim to progress: Knowledge of science outstrips capacity for control. We have too many men of science, too few men of God. The world has achieved brilliance without wisdom, power without conscience. We are a world of nuclear giants and ethical infants." War seems to be the direction of our world. Christ warned His followers that in the last days there would be wars and rumors of wars, climaxing in the Battle of Armageddon.

The first seal brought dominion, the second brings division. There is going to be war, and the Bible says men are going to hate one another. They will kill each other. And it will not simply be nation fighting against nation, but with the spirit of hatred brought by the Antichrist inflaming men's hearts, it will be man against man and brother against brother. Imagine the confusion and consternation. The church will have been taken out of this world, and there will be nothing to hold back the power of evil in mankind. Already we live in a world heavily armed and deeply divided, and without the preserving and reconciling ministry of the church, the swords of this world will drip with blood as men are unrestrained. Some will refuse to go along with the Beast, and they will be slaughtered. There will be dead bodies lying in the streets, the stench of death in the air, and the groaning of suffering everywhere.

The Third Seal: Deprivation

"And when he had opened the third seal, I heard the third beast say, Come and see. And I beheld, and lo a black horse; and he that sat on him had a pair of balances in his hand. And I heard a voice in the midst of the four beasts say, A measure of wheat for a penny, and three measures of barley for a penny; and see thou hurt not the oil and the wine" (vv. 5-6). The third horse will bring a time of famine. The terror of balances represents rationing. People are going to be without the necessities of life. Wholesale starvation is going to take over because famine invariably follows war. When the strong men go off to die and the country's resources are poured into armaments, the availability of food drops while prices soar.

A measure of wheat is what it takes to make one meal. A penny, or denarii, was one day's wages. So literally what is meant is that a man would have to work all day just to get enough food for one meal. Already much of the world lives in perpetual hunger, although we usually don't notice it here in the United States because we are surrounded by plenty. But a famine of an unprecedented scale is coming. The very necessities of life will be rationed.

The Fourth Seal: Death

"And when he opened the fourth seal, I heard the voice of the fourth beast say, Come and see. And I looked, and behold a pale horse" (vv. 7-8). The word *pale* is actually a root word for *green*. It means a sickly green, that of decay, rottenness and gangrene. It's a ghastly yellow-green, the color of death.

"And his name that sat on him was Death, and Hell followed with him. And power was given unto them over the fourth part of the earth, to kill with the sword, and with hunger, and with death, and with the beasts of the earth" (v. 8). The effect of these four horsemen is that twenty-five percent of the people on earth will die. If the Tribulation were to happen soon, that would mean more than one billion people would perish. Being killed with the beasts of the field may mean diseases spread through animals, since the word *death* can also be translated "pestilence." In fourteenth century Europe, one third of the population died because of the bubonic plague, spread by rats. There is a chain of events here that can be traced: The Antichrist comes with dominion and war, which causes division and famine, which brings deprivation and death to a

71

billion people. And hell follows close behind death. Death receives the bodies, but hell receives the souls. After death and hell comes judgment, and then the eternal lake of fire. And no one will be able to escape. What a terrible, gloomy message Revelation holds for those who reject God.

The Fifth Seal: Determination

And when he had opened the fifth seal, I saw under the altar the souls of them that were slain for the word of God, and for the testimony which they held: and they cried with a loud voice, saying, How long, O Lord, holy and true, dost thou not judge and avenge our blood on them that dwell on the earth? And white robes were given unto every one of them; and it was said unto them, that they should rest yet for a little season, until their fellow servants also and their brethren, that should be killed as they were, should be fulfilled. (vv. 9-11)

God has determined to avenge this world. Here are the martyrs for the faith saying, "Lord, why don't you do something?" And God replies, "Just a little while; I am waiting for a few more." You see, there are going to be some people who come to Christ during the Tribulation, and they will refuse the mark of the Beast and will be guillotined. They have died as a sacrifice unto the Lord, and are crying out for God to not let them die in vain. But God knows what he is doing, so He asks them to wait.

The Sixth Seal: Disruption

And I beheld when he had opened the sixth seal, and, lo, there was a great earthquake; and the sun became black as sackcloth of hair, and the moon became as blood; and the stars of heaven fell unto the earth, even as a fig tree casteth her untimely figs, when she is shaken of a mighty wind. And the heaven departed as a scroll when it is rolled together; and every mountain and island were moved out of their places. (vv. 12-14)

Everything is disrupted; something cataclysmic happens and all nature is upset. The Bible tells us that all nature is held together by Christ, and it is as though He allows things to fall apart all at once. Imagine a worldwide disaster so bad that mountains and islands were knocked out of place! The earth itself is going to be in uproar over the control of Satan.

This sort of disruption will cause men to pray so as to escape from the wrath of God. All the great men and kings of the earth "hid themselves in the dens and in the rocks of the mountains; and said to the mountains and rocks, Fall on us, and hide us from the face of him that sitteth on the throne, and from the wrath of the Lamb: for the great day of his wrath is come; and who shall be able to stand?" (vv. 15-17). In their hearts, all men know there is a God. In a time of crisis, they fear Him. As their world falls apart, they can only hide from God. They know of no other answer.

But no Christian will want to hide from Jesus Christ. First Thessalonians 1:10 tells us that we have been delivered from the wrath to come, and 5:9 says that "God hath not appointed us to wrath, but to obtain *salvation* by our Lord Jesus Christ." There is a terrible time coming to earth, a time unlike any that has ever preceded it. But those who love Jesus Christ will be taken out of that terrible time and will spend eternity worshipping in His presence.

APPLICATION

1. What is the significance of the first horseman in Revelation 6? How is this conqueror different from Jesus coming on His horse in Revelation 19:11-16? According to 2 Thessalonians 2:9-10, why is it some people will not be able to understand the times they are experiencing?

2. Why does the first horseman (dominion) lead to the second horseman (division)? Who do you think would not want to submit to the world leader?

3. What do the balances of the third horseman represent? What do you suppose is meant by the phrase "but hurt not the oil and the wine" in verse 6?

4. Why does God allow the kind of death spelled out in verse 8?

5. Who is it that is under the altar in verse 9? How did they die? What do they ask for?

6. How are we, as Christians, to respond to these coming tragedies? How should we live in light of what we know will happen in the future? If Jesus came tonight, would you be ready?

7. Have you ever known a person who really had a sense of "living for the future"? Have you met a Christian who seemed to live in light of the fact that Christ could return at any moment? What was different about that person's life?

8. What do the following verses have to say about Christians and the Tribulation?

   Romans 5:9

   Romans 8:1

   1 Thessalonians 5:1-11

   2 Thessalonians 1:3-10

9. Many Old Testament Scriptures speak of the end times. Read Ezekiel 20:37-38. What do you think is the symbol for the Tribulation? What does Daniel say about the Tribulation in Daniel 8:23-25? What more does Daniel teach us in Daniel 9:25-27 and 12:1-4?

IT'S UP TO YOU

Read the following passages, then write "a Christian manifesto" that clarifies the Christian's responsibility in our world. (Daniel 12:1-3; Matthew 28:19-20; Romans 1:15-16; 2 Timothy 4:1-5)

Chapter 8

PEACE IN THE MIDST OF STORM

OVERVIEW

During the Tribulation, some people will come to know Christ. In this chapter we will take a look at those who come to God in the last days.

INTRODUCTION • REVELATION 7

Revelation 7 is a parenthetical chapter. The Great Tribulation will have already begun upon the earth, yet in that time there will be a special group of people with whom God is dealing. There will be people saved during the Tribulation. Even with the church out of the world, there will be people saved. What an example of the wonderful grace of God!

DISCUSSION

"And after these things I saw four angels" (Revelation 7:1). Don't sentimentalize angels. Don't try to explain them away. Don't discount the reality of Satan's demonic angels, either. That is what the Sadducees did, and Christ rebuked them for their unbelief. The angels seek to minister to us; the demons want to murder us. We must not misunderstand either of them.

Angels are still ministering today. They seem to appear in certain times of great crisis. During the Tribulation Period, angels are going to have a distinctive ministry: "I saw four angels standing on the four corners of the earth, holding the four winds of the earth, that the wind should not blow on the earth, nor on the sea, nor on any tree" (v. 1). So what does that mean?

The Symbolism of Scripture

People have asked the question, "Do I interpret the Bible symbolically or literally?" My answer is always, "Yes!" We believe the Bible is literal truth, and the Apostle John certainly tried to explain complex, sometimes overwhelming events and concepts literally. He attempted to describe what he saw. At the same time, the Holy Spirit certainly communicated in symbolic ways in Scripture.

When John says he saw angels standing on the four corners of the earth, he doesn't mean he believes the earth to be flat and square. That is simply an idiom for the four directions on a compass: north, south, east, and west. John literally says he saw angels from the four "wings" of the world, which is to say, the four quadrants of the globe. The angels are holding back the wind. Is that literal wind or symbolic wind? How can one know? The Bible is full of symbolism, so often things mean something more than the literal description. The Bible says in Revelation 1 that God sent and "signified" the book by his angel to the servant John. *Signified* means "full of symbols," and Revelation is certainly full of symbols. The symbolic language does not do away with the literal interpretation. Each symbol has a literal meaning. One must find what the symbol stands for and believe in it.

So if the Bible describes Satan as a dragon, that does not mean there is not a literal devil. There is a literal devil, and if God wants to use the symbolism of a dragon to describe him, that may simply help us to understand the truth better. Symbolism does not do away with literal interpretation. So a study of prophecy will reveal that "wind" stands for judgment. For example, Proverbs 1:27 says, "When your fear cometh as desolation, and your destruction cometh as a whirlwind; when distress and anguish come upon you." Winds represent distress, anguish, and destruction blowing upon the earth.

So in Revelation 7 John tells of seeing four angels holding back this destruction and anguish on the earth. They seem to be holding back these winds so they cannot blow, because God has something He must do first. For the moment, God restrains His wrath.

The Sealed in Scripture

"And I saw another angel ascending from the east, having the seal of the living God" (v. 2). I believe the seal is the Holy Spirit of God. The Bible says that after you are saved, you are sealed with the Holy Spirit. That is what is unique about you, brother and sister: The Spirit of the Almighty God resides in you. You formerly were dead to God, but now you have been made alive through the Holy Spirit. God has sealed you, placed His mark upon you, by giving you the Holy Spirit.

"And he cried with a loud voice to the four angels, to whom it was given to hurt the earth and the sea, saying, Hurt not the earth, neither the sea, nor the trees, till we have sealed the servants of our God in their foreheads" (vv. 2-3). Now these angels are keeping the time of Tribulation from hurting the earth, and they are holding that time off so that God's people can be sealed, or marked, on the forehead. I do not think that necessarily means the Christians will literally have letters on their heads, but that they will have a true knowledge of God. The term *seal* speaks of the impartation of truth by the Holy Spirit after the angel bears this message.

The Saved of Israel

And I heard the number of them which were sealed: and there were sealed an hundred and forty and four thousand of all the tribes of the children of Israel. Of the tribe of Judah were sealed twelve thousand. Of the tribe of Reuben were sealed twelve thousand. Of the tribe of Gad were sealed twelve thousand. Of the tribe of Asher were sealed twelve thousand. Of the tribe of Nephtali were sealed twelve thousand. Of the tribe of Manasseh were sealed twelve thousand. Of the tribe of Simeon were sealed twelve thousand. Of the tribe of Levi were sealed twelve thousand. Of the tribe of Issachar were sealed twelve thousand. Of the tribe of Zebulun were sealed twelve thousand. Of the tribe of Joseph were sealed twelve thousand. Of the tribe of Benjamin were sealed twelve thousand. (vv. 4-8)

You will notice the tribe of Dan was left out of this list because Dan was a tribe guilty of idolatry. Therefore, their name was blotted out, and the half-tribe of Joseph's son Manasseh brought in.

God is not finished with the Jews. Scripture teaches that God has 144,000 elect Jews who are going to be his special messengers during this time. They will be like 144,000 Apostle Pauls going up and down the land proclaiming the truth of God and explaining the Great Tribulation. The devil will hate this group so much that, were it not for the protecting hand of God, they would be annihilated by Satan.

Today there are many groups who claim to be the 144,000. Some people keep the Sabbath on Saturday and claim that worshipping on Sunday is the mark of the Beast! Jehovah's Witnesses believe their church makes up the 144,000, but they are never sure which ones are in and which are out, so they keep knocking on doors to try and earn their way into that select group. There is another group called "the flying roll" who think their little group represents the 144,000. And there are mainstream Methodists and Presbyterians who say that the 144,000 simply represent the church. They consider the church the "spiritual Israel."

But God is still dealing with the literal Israel, and there is no reason when reading this to believe otherwise. There is nothing in Revelation 7 to make one think this is not literally 144,000 Jews. So if anybody tells you they are part of the 144,000, just ask them what tribe they are from, since the Bible makes a big deal of mentioning each tribe. These are the Jews, God's chosen people. God still has a covenant to keep with Israel. He has kept them for ages. You never see a Hittite any more, and when was the last time you had lunch with a Jebusite? But God has preserved His people, the Jews. Nebuchadnezzar tried to destroy them, Caesar tried to make them disappear, Hitler tried to wipe them off the face of the earth. But God has kept His people.

Paul tells us in Romans 11:25-27 that he does not want his brethren to be ignorant of what he calls "this mystery...that blindness in part is happened to Israel, until the fullness of the Gentiles be come in. And so all Israel shall be saved: as it is written, There shall come out of Zion the Deliverer, and shall turn away ungodliness from Jacob: for this is my covenant unto them, when I shall take away their sins." The Jewish nation is spiritually blind. That is why they missed their Messiah. But God is preserving them to save them. The church is not "spiritual Israel," since the church would never be called "Jacob." Paul says that Jews—real, fleshly Jews—will be led to Christ. According to Revelation 7 they will go through the Tribulation Period, which the Scriptures refer to as "the time of Jacob's trouble," but many shall be saved during it.

The Salvation of Many

After this I beheld, and, lo, a great multitude, which no man could number, of all nations, and kindreds, and people, and tongues, stood before the throne, and before the Lamb, clothed with white robes, and palms in their hands; and cried with a loud voice, saying, Salvation to our God which sitteth upon the throne, and unto the Lamb. (Revelation 7:9-10)

Now these verses are clearly not talking about the Jews. John has already described 144,000 Jews; now he describes a great host of Gentiles who will be saved by the testimony of those 144,000 sealed believers.

A fair question to ask is, "What will happen to all these new believers?" I think they will all be martyred. The Antichrist will be at war with the truth, so he will attempt to squash any attempt at preaching the gospel. They will not worship the Beast and they will not take his mark, so they will be unable to buy or sell. I believe many will die as martyrs, and of course some will perish during the wars and pestilences of the Tribulation. And since this scene seems to take place in heaven, with God wiping away all tears from their eyes, I think it speaks of martyrdom. Here is a vast horde of people from every kindred, tribe, and tongue. Too many to count! But all have turned to Christ, and given up their lives for their decision.

Many people on earth will continue to reject the truth. Even people in churches, when they see their Christian friends disappear in the Rapture, will fail to believe the truth. In 2 Thessalonians 2:9-12 we read about the deception the Antichrist is going to use to keep people from understanding the truth:

Even him, whose coming is after the working of Satan with all power and signs and lying wonders, and with all deceivableness of unrighteousness in them that perish; because they received not the love of the truth, that they might be saved. And for this cause God shall send them strong delusion, that they should believe a lie:

that they all might be damned who believed not the truth, but had pleasure in unrighteousness.

Satan will make people believe that black is white. That way they will not recognize the Antichrist. And God will send them a strong delusion as part of His judgment. You see, Jesus was the Truth. The Antichrist is the lie. People have heard that but choose not to believe it. They want to take pleasure in their sin; they want to choose error. So they have chosen sin; they have chosen to be damned. That is why the Lord said that men hate the light. They will not come to the light because their deeds are evil. Their sin keeps them from believing. And yet, in the mercy of God, a vast multitude will hear the truth and embrace it during the Great Tribulation.

The Scene in Heaven

> *And all the angels stood round about the throne, and about the elders and the four beasts, and fell before the throne on their faces and worshiped God, saying, Amen: Blessing, and glory, and wisdom, and thanksgiving, and honor, and power, and might, be unto our God for ever and ever. Amen.* (Revelation 7:11-12)

The angels get all excited about the grace and mercy of God. He stoops to save people who do not deserve salvation, because He is infinitely loving. Heaven is full of people recognizing their unworthiness and praising God for His mercy.

> *And one of the elders answered, saying unto me... These are they which came out of great tribulation, and have washed their robes, and made them white in the blood of the Lamb. Therefore are they before the throne of God and serve him day and night in his temple: and he that sitteth on the throne shall dwell among them. They shall hunger no more, neither thirst any more; neither shall the sun light on them, nor any heat. For the Lamb which is in the midst of the throne shall feed them, and shall lead them unto living fountains of waters: and God shall wipe away all tears from their eyes.* (vv. 13-17)

These verses make it abundantly clear. This horde of people went through extremely difficult times during the Tribulation, suffering hunger, thirst, and persecution. They ended up as martyrs for the Lord. They understand how much they have been forgiven, and they willingly serve out of their love for Him. And the picture John gives us of those people in heaven is one of being tenderly cared for by a loving God who comforts them, keeps them, and dwells among them.

APPLICATION

1. What symbolism in the Scriptures do you most appreciate? (For example, the Good Shepherd, the Rock of our Salvation, etc.) What symbolism do you not understand?

2. Why do you suppose the Holy Spirit allowed the message of Revelation to be communicated symbolically rather than literally? Do you ever use symbolic language? What does it add to your communication?

3. In Revelation 7:3-8, the author speaks of many people being "sealed." What does it mean to be sealed? Ephesians 1:13-14 use the same Greek word. What do those verses tell us? What does Ephesians 4:30 reveal? Read 2 Corinthians 1:21-22. What is the seal we have?

4. The word translated *seal* or *deposit* was the word used when a man became engaged to a woman. He gave her a ring as a promise that he would fulfill his vow and as a sign to others that she belonged to someone. How is the sealing of Christians similar to that ancient custom?

5. Using our study of numbers in an earlier chapter, what is the significance of the number 144,000?

6. Why does it best make sense to assume the 144,000 are believing Jews? Why can't we simply substitute "the church" for "Israel" in the New Testament letters?

7. From your own reading and study, what is significant about the Jewish nation? Why did they not accept Jesus as the Messiah initially? Why will so many turn to Him at the end times?

8. In your own words how would you describe God's actions toward the martyrs in Revelation 7:14-17? How do the martyrs respond to God?

WHAT'S YOUR STORY?

Write out your testimony. Tell what your life was like before you met Jesus, how you were introduced to the Lord, what convinced you to turn your life over to Him, and what has happened in your life since you became a Christian.

Chapter 9

THE MYSTERIOUS MULTITUDE

OVERVIEW

The worship of the 144,000 Jews saved during the Tribulation shows us what it will be like to worship God in heaven.

INTRODUCTION • REVELATION 7:9-17

You already know that there is a time coming such as our world has never seen. The Bible calls it "the time of Jacob's trouble," and Jesus referred to it as "the Great Tribulation." This Tribulation Period is going to take place sometime before Christ comes back to this earth to reign. There will be seven years of terrible tribulation. It will be a time of tyranny and persecution; a time when nature itself will be thrown out of balance, demons will infest the world, and a thoroughly evil man, the Antichrist, will rule the earth. It will be the time of Jacob's trouble, but the Bible says the Jewish nation will be saved out of it. During this time, the nation of Israel will come to know that Jesus Christ is King of Kings and Lord of Lords, and they will receive Him as their Savior.

DISCUSSION

The People

> *In the midst of this tribulation is a great multitude of people. I beheld, and, lo, a great multitude, which no man could number, of all nations, and kindreds, and people, and tongues, stood before the throne, and before the Lamb, clothed with white robes, and palms in their hands; and cried with a loud voice, saying, Salvation to our God which sitteth upon the throne, and unto the Lamb...and one of the elders answered, saying unto me, What are these which are arrayed in white robes? and whence came they? And I said unto him, Sir, thou knowest. And he said to me, These are they which came out of great tribulation, and have washed their robes, and made them white in the blood of the Lamb.* (Revelation 7:9-10, 13-14)

What a mysterious multitude! Somehow they have come out of the Tribulation, have been washed whiter than snow, and are now in heaven, encircling the throne.

Saved

These people have been washed in the blood of the Lamb and are in heaven praising the Lord, so we know that they are saved. The question is, how did they come to know Christ in the midst of the Great Tribulation?

Remember that there were 144,000 Jews who had turned to the Lord Jesus and had received God's protective seal. So we know that, even with all sorts of evil and wickedness going unrestrained, some are still seeing the truth and accepting Christ as their personal Savior. Remember, God is not finished with the nation of Israel. He has a purpose that will be fulfilled. You can read all about the future of Israel in Romans 9-11. The nation of Israel is going to be restored spiritually and politically, and the Jews will be God's prophets in the last days, bringing the truth to the nations.

Servants

Revelation 7:3 calls them the "servants of our God." These 144,000 Jews will be sealed by God as a sign of preservation. God's seal is His authority, and God is going to put His preservation, protection, power, and authority on those Jews who believe in His

Son. Then they are going to evangelize the world, preaching the glorious Gospel of Jesus Christ. Do you see the grace of God at work? He will pull out the church at the start of the Tribulation, only to have their work taken up by His chosen people. The world will once again be blessed by the fruit of Israel. The Prophet Isaiah spoke of this time when he said, "Arise, shine; for thy light is come, and the glory of the LORD is risen upon thee. For, behold, darkness shall cover the earth, and gross darkness the people: but the LORD shall arise upon thee, and His glory shall be seen upon thee. And the Gentiles shall come to thy light, and kings to the brightness of thy rising" (Isaiah 60:1-3). In the midst of the worst darkness, a light once again shines forth from the nation of Israel.

Great nations are going to hear the Gospel. The greatest gathering of souls is yet in the future. It will take place, believe it or not, after the church has been taken out of this world. The greatest evangelistic harvest the world has ever seen will take place during the Tribulation, when 144,000 Messianic Jews preach the good news of the Gospel of Jesus Christ. Matthew 24:14 tells us that the Gospel will be preached in all the nations, and then the end shall come. The end of what? The end of the Great Tribulation. There will be a worldwide witness where many Gentiles of many nations and races receive Christ. And they will all have been won by these Jewish witnesses.

The Place

Recall that, in Revelation 5, there was a throne in heaven with a rainbow around it that looked like an emerald. Now, after the 144,000 Jews have preached the Gospel in the world, there is a great multitude of people who have believed. They are before the throne. Revelation 7:9 is a heavenly scene, with a great multitude that no man can number worshipping God. They are there before the throne because they have given their lives for their faith.

Around The Throne

Notice that all these people in this multitude are crowding around the throne of God, clothed in white with palm leaves in their hands as a sign of peace, and they are all shouting in loud voices, "Salvation to our God!" When they do that, the elders and the four created beings fall on their faces before Him. This kind of worship would make some Christians nervous. Shouting to God?

Most of us have been conditioned not to make any noise in church. Waving palm branches? Most of us associate that with some Palm Sunday ritual in the Roman Catholic Church. Falling on your face? That would happen only if you fell asleep in a prayer meeting!

Encircled with Worship

But you know, it should be exciting to worship God. If being forgiven of your sins and having a place reserved for you in heaven doesn't excite you, something is wrong with your soul. These people are so excited about what they have been saved from, they can't help but shout. When was the last time you got so excited about being saved you had to shout? They are using the Old Testament symbol of palm branches as a sign of glory. In John 12:12 we read, "People that were come to the feast, when they heard that Jesus was coming to Jerusalem, took branches of palm trees, and went forth to meet him, and cried, Hosanna: Blessed is the King of Israel that cometh in the name of the Lord." To wave palm branches was symbolic of the peace and joy God brings, and the blessedness of knowing God is in control of events. It was a way of showing the thrill of being with God. Compare it to when you are sitting in an end zone, and your team scores the winning touchdown in the last minute of the game. You throw your arms in the air and shout for joy. How much more exciting is it to know that God has forgiven you of all your sin and has prepared a place for you to be with Him in eternity.

Years ago, the quarterback of the New York Jets, Joe Namath, wrote a book entitled, *I Can't Wait Until Tomorrow, 'Cause I Get Better Looking Every Day.* Now I don't get better every day on the outside, but I should be getting more like Jesus every day on the inside. Imagine how our worship would change if we couldn't wait to be with God each day. Though our outward man perish, our inward man is renewed day by day. It is exciting being a Christian, and these people in heaven are so excited, they have to shout and wave and give glory to God. Revelation tells us that the elders praise God, the creatures praise God, even the angels give praise to God for what He has done. As the psalmist said, "Let everything that hath breath praise the Lord."

The Persecution

Note that in Revelation 7:14 the elder says, "These are they which came out of great tribulation, and have washed their robes, and made them white in the blood of the Lamb." This multitude was persecuted while they were down here on earth. They are God's majestic martyrs, for they paid for their faith with their lives. When they got saved, they refused to take the mark of the Beast, so they were put to death. That is why Revelation 6:9 reads, "When he had opened the fifth seal, I saw under the altar the souls of them that were slain for the word of God, and for the testimony which they held."

During the Tribulation many are going to be murdered who believe the Word of God. Like the many martyrs of the past or the missionary martyrs of our own day, they will be tortured and killed for their faith.

The Privilege

Revelation 7:15 tells us that this multitude who have been saved "are before the throne of God, and serve him day and night in his temple: and he that sitteth on the throne shall dwell among them." What a privilege is theirs. These saints who have been saved in the Tribulation now serve God continually. That might not immediately seem important to you, but remember that during the Old Testament times, only the priests could serve in the temple. The common man was left outside. But now there is a temple in glory, and every person from every tribe and nation can serve the Lord. What a privilege that will be!

And don't think that when we get to heaven, we will simply sit around on fluffy clouds plucking harps. We will be actively serving God. "His servants shall serve Him," says in Revelation 22:3. We will all be singing and praising God, even those of us here on earth who can't really sing or who struggle with how to really praise Him. Someday that privilege will be ours, Christian.

The Provision

"They shall hunger no more, neither thirst any more, neither shall the sun light upon them, nor any heat. For the Lamb which is in the midst of the throne shall feed them and shall lead them into living fountains of waters" (Revelation 7:16-17). The people in this multitude have suffered from hunger. They have been thirsty. The powers on earth kept them from being able to purchase adequate food and water. They have been locked up in some cases, away from sunlight, or have hidden in dark places. They have been exposed to the heat and the cold. But in heaven, God is going to provide for all their needs. They will have come through difficult times, but the Lord will be taking care of them for eternity.

You never think of the sheep taking the place of the shepherd, but that's what this passage says. "The Lamb which is in the midst of the throne shall feed them, and shall lead them." The Lamb will become the Shepherd, caring for His flock and being their leader. He will dry the tears of those who have suffered greatly for their faith during the Tribulation. And that multitude will sing and shout and dance about, excited that the Lord has delivered them from that terrible time.

There was a car accident close to my church recently, and I became so intent on watching the activity as I drove by that I almost caused another accident by hitting the car in front of me! The same thing can happen in a study of prophecy. You can get so interested in the symbolic meaning of the details, can get all wrapped up in determining the number of horns on all the beasts, that you miss the larger point. You can be watching the parts of the Revelation intently and suddenly have a collision with destiny because you have never made a decision for Christ yourself. Don't think you can put off your decision until the world enters the Great Tribulation, for the Bible clearly says that those who wait will be given a strong delusion so that they will be unable to accept the truth. They will be deceived by the Antichrist, take the mark of the Beast, and spend eternity separated from God. All of the events in Revelation are going to come to pass shortly. Make sure you are ready for eternity and have been made white in the blood of the Lamb.

APPLICATION

1. In this passage, we see people waving palm branches, crying out with a loud voice, and falling on their faces before God. What is the significance of the palm branches? Why were the people shouting out their praise to God? Why were they falling down on their faces?

2. Why does God seems nearer at some times than others? What does the psalmist mean in Psalm 22:3? How can we experience the presence of God in a more meaningful way?

3. What principles of worship do you glean from Romans 1: 18-25? What is "plain" to people (vv. 19-20)? What implication does that have for all people? What have most people chosen to worship instead (vv. 21-23)? What is the result of that choice (vv. 24-32)?

WORSHIP OF GOD

How could we make our worship more like that of heaven?

Chapter 10

AN INVASION FROM HELL

OVERVIEW

A study of Revelation 8 and 9 reveals what the world will be like when Satan really takes over.

INTRODUCTION • REVELATION 8:1-9:11

The Great Tribulation is described in Revelation 6 as a series of judgments that occur as a seven-sealed scroll is unrolled. As each seal is broken, a judgment is read out. One seal is yet to be broken, the last and by far the most terrible of the horrors that unfold. The last seal is called the trumpet judgment, because within the seventh seal are seven trumpets that will sound.

DISCUSSION

"And when he had opened the seventh seal, there was silence in heaven about the space of half an hour" (Revelation 8:1). This is probably the longest silence heaven has ever known. Usually it is filled with music and worship and praise to God continually ascending to His throne. But here is a time when all heaven holds its breath. The seventh seal is so awesome and terrifying that no one in heaven dares breathe a word.

"And I saw the seven angels which stood before God; and to them were given seven trumpets" (v. 2). In Scripture a trumpet is symbolic of several things. Often a trumpet stands for alarm. It was used to call people to war. However, it also was used as a signal that God was getting ready to intervene in the affairs of men. Often a trumpet sounds as some miraculous work of God happens.

The Judgment Fire

> *And another angel came and stood at the altar, having a golden censer; and there was given unto him much incense, that he should offer it with the prayers of all saints upon the golden altar which was before the throne. And the smoke of the incense, which came with the prayers of the saints, ascended up before God out of the angel's hand. And the angel took the censer, and filled it with fire of the altar, and cast it into the earth: and there were voices, and thunderings, and lightnings, and an earthquake. (vv. 3-5)*

A censer is used to burn incense, and in this case the incense is mixed with all the prayers of God's people which rise to the Lord on High. Many times we think that perhaps He has forgotten the prayers of His people, but He has not. He has been saving them for thousands of years, and they are about to be answered. For when the last trumpet sounds, the kingdoms of this world will become the kingdom of Jesus Christ.

Note that the angel casts the fire from the altar into the earth. The altar is where the sacrifice was made, so it is a place of both salvation and judgment. When Christ died on Calvary, He offered us salvation. But he also took the fires of God's judgment onto Himself. So the picture here is of an impenitent world, refusing to bow before God, and having the fire from that altar flung onto it. As the prayers of the saints ascend, the judgment of God descends. And the voices and thunderings are the frightened forebodings of something terrible about to happen on earth.

The Judgment of the Physical World

The first trumpet brings hail and fire onto the earth, and one third of the greenery on earth is destroyed. That is God's judgment upon all vegetation. The second brings a burning destruction of the sea, and one third of all sea creatures die and ships are destroyed. That is God's judgment against the sea. The third brings a comet to the earth which poisons one third of the water supply. That is God's judgment concerning the waters. Then the fourth trumpet sounds, darkening the skies. That is God's judgment against the heavens. You can theorize all you want about nuclear war, nuclear fallout, or nuclear winter, but the fact is John records incredible devastation on earth due to God's judgment on the natural world. However, it will get much worse when God's judgment is made against mankind. For as bad as those events are, John "heard an angel flying through the midst of heaven, saying with a loud voice, Woe, woe, woe, to the inhabiters of the earth by reason of the other voices of the trumpet of the three angels, which are yet to sound" (v. 13).

The Judgment of Man

"And the fifth angel sounded, and I saw a star fall from heaven unto the earth: and to him was given the key of the bottomless pit" (Revelation 9:1). The devil has been momentarily unleashed during the Great Tribulation. Hell has had a holiday. Satan is ruling the earth and his demons infesting the world. But Satan has already fallen. He was originally called the sun of the morning, the bright and morning star. But he turned against God and was cast out of heaven. He is the fallen star. And John sees him with a key to the bottomless pit in his hand.

The bottomless pit is the abyss, the place where Satan will be confined during the Millennium. It is a place of incarceration that holds extremely vile and malevolent spirits. Jesus sent some spirits to that pit when He cast them out of men. And now God has allowed Satan to have the key to unleash his evil friends and let all demonic spirits free to invade the earth. The devil has longed to have that key, and now he has the authority to let loose unspeakable evil upon the earth. There are eleven things to notice about how the Holy Spirit describes these demon spirits.

Infernal

"And he opened the bottomless pit; and there arose a smoke out of the pit, as the smoke of a great furnace; and the sun and the air were darkened by reason of the smoke from the pit. And there came out of the smoke locusts upon the earth" (vv 2-3). These demons are as locusts, which in the Middle East sometimes cover the earth in great clouds. Swarming billions of them cross the face of the earth, actually darkening the skies. They are hellish, diabolical, fiendish beings let loose to invade the earth.

Insatiable

"And unto them was given power, as the scorpions of the earth have power. And it was commanded them that they should not hurt the grass of the earth, neither any green things, neither any tree; but only those men which have not the seal of God in their foreheads" (vv. 3-4). Remember that there are 144,000 Jews on earth who have turned to Christ and received the protecting seal of God in their foreheads. These demons cannot hurt them. But they will have an insatiable appetite to torment others.

When a plague of locusts hits an area, they will eat everything in sight. Every blade of grass, every leaf on a tree, every flower and stalk of grain. They have even been known to strip the bark from trees. They are insatiable, eating and eating and eating. That is how these demons will be, except they will attack men and women rather than green plants.

Intolerable

"And to them it was given that they should not kill them, but that they should be tormented five months: and their torment was as the torment of a scorpion, when he striketh a man" (v. 5). The devil loves to torment people. He wants to see people suffer, so he will send out his demonic forces to cause pain and torment on the earth.

I was once stung by a scorpion on my hands, and I got sick with nausea, swollen glands under my arms, and pain so bad I thought I would pass out. And God's Word says that millions and millions of demons, like great swarms of locusts, will be inflicting that sort of pain upon mankind. It will be so bad, according to verse 6, that men will seek death "and shall desire to die, and death will flee from them." There will be no escape from these demons.

Irresistible

"And the shapes of the locusts were like unto horses prepared unto battle" (v. 7). This symbolizes their rapid progress. Like a steed charging over the ground, they will stop at nothing. No one will be able to resist them as they go marching on. Satan's evil forces, streaming out of their vile pit, cover the land with pain.

Invincible

"And on their heads were as it were crowns like gold" (v. 7). The crowns signify that Satan and his cohorts are in control. They are ruling the world for a short while. The devil has the keys and is on the throne doing what he has always wanted to do. He has always desired a crown, the chance to proclaim himself king. There have been many who would like to have him wear that crown. So for a while he rules the world, but woe to those who remain on the earth when that takes place.

Intelligent

"And their faces were as the faces of men" (v. 7). In the Bible, the face of a man is symbolic of intelligence. You see, these are not literal, ordinary locusts. They are intelligent beings with a very cunning plan. Scripture tells us that the devil was more subtle than any beast of the field, and he has imparted that intelligence to his followers. He has always magnified human wisdom. He always appeals to reason rather than revelation. That is why he works so hard in our culture to get us to scientifically reason away God. His appeal is to the head, not the heart, and because of this men are going to receive judgment from God.

Insidious

"And they had hair as the hair of women, and their teeth were as the teeth of lions" (v. 8). The Bible says that a woman's hair is given to her for her glory. It is a beautiful thing, given by God as a crown to women. But these demons are going to use that as a trap. They will appear to be very alluring. They will use their appearance to seduce mankind. But they will have teeth like lions, ready to shred and devour those they come upon. Once a lion closes his jaws, it is nearly impossible to force them open. So once a demon has trapped someone, that person will remain trapped. These evil spirits are sneaky and insidious. They appear at first to be attractive and beautiful, but really they are harmful and destructive.

Insensitive

"And they had breastplates, as it were breastplates of iron" (v. 9); that is, they are heartless. No matter how much people shriek and groan, these demons will not be moved. They are impervious to the workings of man, so it won't matter what a doctor or a psychiatrist or a military officer orders. They will not be moved from their course of action. They have breastplates of iron and are implacable.

Inescapable

"And the sound of their wings was as the sound of chariots of many horses running to battle" (v. 9). They will be everywhere. There will be no escape. They will be flying about and there will be no one who can outrun them, no place to hide. These demons will only be stopped after they have run their course. The passage says they will be set free for five months, which is the life of a locust, so they will simply do what they have come to do regardless of any action taken against them.

Injurious

"And they had tails like unto scorpions, and there were stings in their tails: and their power was to hurt men five months" (v. 10). The devil wants to deceive people into thinking he will help them, but Satan is a liar, the father of all liars, according to Jesus. Christ once said, "When he lies, he speaks his native tongue." If people would only realize that when they follow the devil, they are chasing after one who only wants to hurt them. When they follow the Lord, He wants to help and heal them. The devil is no friend, but people will be fooled into following him, and he and his demon spirits will hurt everyone on earth for five months.

Indivisible

"And they had a king over them, which is the angel of the bottomless pit, whose name in the Hebrew tongue is Abaddon, but in the Greek tongue hath his name Apollyon" (v. 11). All of these demons will be organized and will know precisely what they are to do. And their leader's name, translated, is "Destroyer." He organizes them to destroy mankind, and his name is given in both Hebrew and Greek because he will make sure they attack both Jews and Gentiles who do not have the seal of God on their forehead.

What do you think America would be like if every prison and jail cell were thrown open and every criminal turned loose in the streets? What if there was no police force to hold them back, and they were organized to make war on the citizenry? As awful as that sounds, it cannot compare to the millions of inhuman demons that will be let loose with the fifth trumpet of the Tribulation.

APPLICATION

1. Why was there silence in heaven in Revelation 8:1? Have you ever been stunned into silence? What could bring about that kind of response from the angels and the dead in Christ?

2. Look at the following verses to see how trumpets were represented in Jewish culture:

   Exodus 19:16-19; 20:18

   Joshua 6:5

   Judges 6:34

1 Samuel 13:3

1 Kings 1:34

Psalm 47:5

Ezekiel 33:2-6

Matthew 24:31

1 Corinthians 15:52

3. What is the significance of the angel throwing the altar fire to the earth?

4. What have you been praying for over a long period of time? How can we know that God hears our prayers and will answer them?

5. Why does God judge the physical world in Revelation 8:7-12?

6. What does Isaiah tell about the roots of Satan in Isaiah 14:12-15? What more do you learn about him in Genesis 3:1-5; Job 2:1-7; John 8:42-47; 2 Corinthians 11:14?

7. What do the following passages reveal about evil spirits?

Deuteronomy 32:17

Matthew 8:28-33

Mark 1:34

Luke 9:1; 10:17

1 Corinthians 10:20-21

1 Timothy 4:1

James 2:19

James 3:14-15

OVERCOMING SATAN

Read Luke 4:1-13. What strategy did Satan use on Jesus? How did Jesus fight back? What strategy does Satan use on you? What steps could you take to fight him?

Chapter 11

A WORLD GONE WILD

OVERVIEW

When the sixth angel blows his trumpet, there will be war on the earth as never before. In this study we will examine Revelation 9 to see the power, the people, and the purpose involved in that destructive time.

INTRODUCTION • REVELATION 9:12-21

There are seven seals that are broken open on the scroll as Christ unrolls it. As those seals break, the Tribulation terrors unfold upon the earth. Out of the seventh seal come seven trumpets, which represent seven judgments. Seven alarming things will take place as the Great Tribulation builds in intensity. As the sixth trumpet sounds, the world goes completely wild.

DISCUSSION

And the sixth angel sounded, and I heard a voice from the four horns of the golden altar which is before God, saying to the sixth angel which had the trumpet, Loose the four angels which are bound in the great river Euphrates. And the four angels were

loosed, which were prepared for an hour, and a day, and a month, and a year, for to slay the third part of men. And the number of the army of the horsemen were two hundred thousand thousand; and I heard the number of them. And thus I saw the horses in the vision, and them that sat on them, having breastplates of fire, and of jacinth, and brimstone: and the heads of the horses were as the heads of lions; and out of their mouths issued fire and smoke and brimstone. By these three was the third part of men killed, by the fire, and by the smoke, and by the brimstone, which issued out of their mouths. For their power is in their mouth and in their tails: for their tails were like unto serpents, and had heads, and with them they do hurt. And the rest of the men which were not killed by these plagues yet repented not of the works of their hands, that they should not worship devils, and idols of gold, and silver, and brass, and stone, and of wood: which neither can see, nor hear, nor walk: neither repented they of their murders, nor of their sorceries, nor of their fornication, nor of their thefts.
(Revelation 9:13-21)

The Sacred Power That Is Involved

Evidently there is a golden altar in heaven, and it has four horns. In Bible prophecy, horns are a symbol of power. The number four is the number of the earth; therefore, a universal power over the earth is residing in heaven. The altar was a place of judgment and redemption, and it was at the Old Testament altar that sin was judged and the animals were slain. The altar was the place where God's fire of wrath fell upon an innocent sacrifice. So this altar is speaking about the power of God—His power in salvation and His power in judgment. The New Testament altar, of course, is the cross of Jesus Christ, the fulfillment of every smoking altar.

What the altar teaches us is that our sins will either be forgiven or they will be judged. That is the message of every altar. Either you will find forgiveness and peace with God through your worship, or you will be judged for your sins. Your sin will be pardoned in Christ, or your sin will be punished in hell. If the fire does not fall upon Jesus, who paid the penalty for your sin, then it will fall upon you. Christ was your substitute, taking your place and paying the penalty for your sins. He took on your punishment, and you must give your life to Him in response.

The altar reveals the mighty power of God. He has power to save or power to judge. There is no other place in this universe to find forgiveness. Only God can judge, and only He can forgive. This altar in Revelation 9 speaks of universal judgment upon the world. Some people have turned to Him and found forgiveness, but those left on earth have rejected Him and will find judgment. Since that altar reveals His power over all the earth, the trumpet tells the whole world it will now be judged by a holy God who has an awful hatred of sin. That is the reason the voice comes from the four horns; it is proclaiming God's judgment.

The Spirit Persons Involved

The voice tells the trumpeter to loose the four angels of the Euphrates. These are four of the most wicked and powerful fallen angels. God has kept them bound until this point in time, for if He did not, the world would no doubt be in tribulation today. Each of these four filthy angels is a prince that rules over an evil empire. They have been restrained by God, kept in the area of the Euphrates.

In Daniel 10:12, when the prophet has prayed and prayed over something, the Lord sends an angel who tells Daniel, "Fear not, Daniel: for from the first day that thou didst set thine heart to understand, and to chasten thyself before thy God, thy words were heard, and I am come for thy words." But in verse 13, Daniel says, "The prince of the kingdom of Persia withstood me one and twenty days." That heavenly messenger admits that Daniel's prayer was heard, but he was held up for twenty-one days by a mighty force called the Prince of Persia: He then tells Daniel that he must "return to fight with the prince of Persia, and when I am gone forth, lo, the prince of Grecia shall come" (Daniel 10:20-21). Persia is now called Iran, and it still has a chief demon as its prince. Greece has an evil spirit leader also. Our problems with Iran are not just against the Ayatollah or the ruling leader. Scripture says we are not just wrestling against flesh and blood, but against principalities and powers in the heavenly places. We are doing battle with the spiritual forces of evil over Iran.

So there are four fallen angels located at the River Euphrates, and they have four worldwide evil kingdoms. Babylon was the first worldwide kingdom, and it began on the River Euphrates. After Babylon came the Persian Empire, followed by Greece, then Rome. All of these great kingdoms were cradled in this area of the world, so it is natural to assume that Satan would put four powerful demons in control of the area. The four great empires of antiquity were each a counterfeit for the kingdom of heaven. And these four demons were somehow bound by God in the Euphrates to keep them from destroying the work of Christ on earth. God now releases them to do their evil work.

The Special Place

The Euphrates River has special meaning. It flowed out of the Garden of Eden at the beginning of the time. It was in that vicinity that Cain killed Abel. It was on its banks that Nimrod began his kingdom, leading to the Tower of Babel. Here was the first prototype of the kingdom of the Antichrist. You see, the Euphrates is both the cradle and the grave of the kingdom of Satan. Rebellion against God began here, and God is moving in a mysterious way to wrap up the history of the world in this place.

The River Euphrates is traditionally the dividing line between the East and the West. God gave to Abraham the Promised Land extending as far as the Euphrates, and the other side of the river is considered the Far East. The Euphrates serves as the dividing line. Archaeologists consider it the birthplace of civilization. It is a special place, and the Lord will use it as the graveyard at the end of time.

The Specific Period

These angels are let loose for a specific period of time: "an hour, and a day, and a month, and a year" (v. 15). That does not mean they will be let loose for three months, although it may seem like that at first reading. But if you look at the original Greek words, what the author is saying is that they will be loosed at a particular time. There is a specific time for them to be unchained, and that time has been prepared for all eternity. It will not happen by chance; it will only occur when the Lord allows it. Those angels are prepared for that very hour, ready to kill one-third of the earth's population.

So we see that, even in tribulation, God is sovereign. Even though there is a world gone wild, nothing is happening by chance. There is no panic in heaven, only plans. Everything will happen according to God's perfect timing. That is why Jesus, when He was on earth, could tell people that when they see the prophecies of the Great Tribulation coming to pass, their redemption is drawing near.

A space shuttle launch was once scuttled because the computer was off by one twenty-fifth of a second. But God is even closer than that. Everything at the end of time will happen in His time, and you can rest assured it will all be perfect. The sixth trumpet will blow at a specific, God-ordained period of time.

The Solemn Purpose

These wicked angels have one very clear purpose: "to slay the third part of men" (v. 15). One third of the remaining population is going to be devastated when the sixth trumpet blows. With the earlier deaths, that means about one half of the earth's population will have perished during this Great Tribulation. The world will be one massive graveyard.

Verse 16 says that there will be an army, coming out of the East, with 200 million men. If you had read that in the first century, you might not have believed it, since there were not 200 million people on the entire planet. During World War II the United States had only twelve million under arms at any one time. Yet more than thirty years ago the Chinese army, an army from the east, announced they had an army of 200 million. And Revelation 16:12 tells us that the River Euphrates is gong to be dried up, that the way might be prepared for the king of the East. For you see, the Antichrist is going to be a Western ruler, and apparently the Eastern rulers will decide at this point to take them on in battle. One third of the world's population will be killed in the ensuing battle.

And since God gave John a vision of the future, he described the weapons of war as best he could. Therefore his description in verses 17 to 19 of fire-breathing horses with breastplates is simply the best way he could express our modern implements of war. It was unlike any horse or army John had ever known. It may very well be a description of some sort of nuclear war. And that terrible war will slay many.

The Stubborn Pride

In the midst of all this destruction, do the people left on earth fall on their faces in humility before God? Do they admit their sin and ask God's forgiveness? No. They remain stubbornly proud and refuse to repent. They insist on rebellion toward God, and continue to worship demons and idols.

Recently we have seen a renewed interest in witchcraft, the occult, parapsychology, astrology, and Satan worship. New Age thinking and earth worship have replaced Sunday School and church attendance in many towns. The secret societies are really just old heresies brought back. Satan was thrown out of heaven for desiring God's place, and he still desires to be worshipped and adored.

The people at this time will continue in their rebellion, even refusing to repent of murder, sorcery, fornication, or theft. Have you noticed the increase in the homicide rate in our country? People will kill over an insult. Life has become cheap. Murder plays out on television every night as entertainment, so as to dull us to the horror of it.

The word translated *sorceries* in verse 21 is the root word from which we get "pharmacy." In other words, people will be using drugs at ever-increasing levels. And people will continue in their fornication, with their minds set on pornography, perversion, and immorality. Personal property will mean nothing, since stealing will be the norm. And as you look this list over, you can see that all of these things are a big part of our culture. It doesn't take much imagination to picture each of them becoming more prevalent in the Great Tribulation. It is coming soon. When that sixth trumpet sounds, the world will go wild. I am glad I won't be here to suffer through it. I will be safe in the arms of my Lord and Savior, Jesus Christ.

APPLICATION

1. How is an Old Testament altar a symbol of salvation? How is it a symbol of judgment? How does Jesus Christ's death on the cross cover over your sins and keep you from judgment?

2. What evidence do we have that God has a specific timetable in mind for the last days? How have you seen God work at a specific time in your own life?

3. Why does God include prophecy in Scripture? What benefit is there to knowing something about the future?

4. Read Daniel 8:1, 15, 17, and 27. What do they reveal about Daniel's reaction to prophecy? What was Daniel's involvement in the communication? What is your reaction when you read prophecy?

5. Why do you suppose people in the last days still won't turn to God and repent of their sin? Have you ever been hardhearted about a sin? How did it affect your life?

6. Where do you see the evil acts in verses 20 and 21 expressed in our own culture?

DOING BATTLE

Who does Paul say is the enemy in Ephesians 6:12? What implication does that have for your life?

Chapter 12

WHEN TIME IS NO MORE

OVERVIEW

In this passage we take a respite from the horror on earth and are reminded by the Lord that all of these events in Revelation, incredible as they are, will take place in the near future.

INTRODUCTION • REVELATION 10

When we studied the seven seals, you will remember that John described the first six seals, then took a respite. He introduced a sort of parenthesis as a break from the horrific event he was observing. Within the seventh seal were seven trumpets, six of which have already blown. Now, before the seventh angel blows his trumpet, the apostle again takes a needed rest from detailing the carnage on earth. Chapter 10 is parenthetical, but very important, as God offers insight before the sounding of the last trumpet.

DISCUSSION

> *And I saw another mighty angel come down from heaven, clothed with a cloud: and a rainbow was upon his head, and his face was as it were the sun, and his feet as pillars of fire: and he had in his hand a little book open: and he set his right foot upon the sea, and his left foot on the earth, and cried, with a loud voice, as when a lion roareth: and when he had cried seven thunders uttered their voices. And when the seven thunders had uttered their voices, I was about to write: and I heard a voice from heaven saying unto me, Seal up those things which the seven thunders uttered, and write them not. And the angel which I saw stand upon the sea and upon the earth lifted up his hand to heaven, and sware by him that liveth for ever and ever, who created heaven, and the things that therein are, and the earth, and the things that therein are, and the sea, and the things which are therein, that there should be time no longer: But in the days of the voice of the seventh angel, when he shall begin to sound, the mystery of God should be finished, as he hath declared to his servants the prophets.* (Revelation 10:1-7)

A Mighty Angel

John begins this passage by describing a mighty angel, Jesus Christ Himself. Don't be bothered that Jesus is described as an angel. In the Old Testament He appears to Abraham as an angel of the Lord on two different occasions. The word translated *angel* simply means "messenger." Jesus is the messenger of the covenant. He is the Lord's mighty messenger.

Isaiah 63:9 reads, "In all their affliction he was afflicted, and the angel of his presence saved them: in his love and in his pity he redeemed them; and he bare them and carried them all the days of old." This beautiful verse once again refers to our Lord Jesus Christ as an angel. God makes His presence real and known to us through the Lord Jesus, His mighty angel.

His Magnificence

There are many other angels, of course, but notice how this particular messenger is described in Revelation 10. He is more magnificent than any other angel. First, his face is as the sun (v. 1). In the first chapter of Revelation, Christ is described as having the countenance of the noonday sun. And at the Transfiguration before Peter, James, and John, "His face did shine as the sun" (Matthew 17:2). When Paul was on the road to Damascus, the Lord Jesus Christ appeared to him and was described as "a light above the brightness of the noon day sun." Malachi called Jesus the "sun of righteousness." He is the bright and morning star, the one resplendent in glory, radiating the shekinah glory of Almighty God.

Second, he has feet like pillars of fire. In Revelation 1:15, Christ is described as having feet like burnished brass, as though they glowed in a fire. Brass is symbolic of judgment, and the feet of Jesus aflame speak of Christ going forth both to purify with fire and judge in righteousness.

Third, notice that he is clothed with a cloud. Clouds in Scripture are the symbols of divine presence. Chapter 1 of Revelation speaks of Christ coming back to this earth on a cloud. Jehovah led Israel across the desert in a pillar of cloud. God spoke out of a cloud at the Transfiguration when He said, "This is my beloved Son, in whom I am well pleased" (Matthew 3:17). The cloud is one more proof that this is Jesus Christ.

Fourth, there is a rainbow upon His head, which speaks of the multicolored splendor of our covenant-keeping Christ. The rainbow is the sign of His covenant. This rainbow upon His brow tells us that Jesus is the peace in the midst of the storm.

His Might

The angel also has in his hand a book (Revelation 10:2), the same book that we saw in chapter 5. Remember, everyone was weeping because there was no one worthy to take the book and open the seals. Then the Lamb stepped forward, took the book, and opened the seals. He alone was worthy to take the title deed to the earth. As you can see, that deed has now been opened. It is no longer sealed up. The Lamb has broken open the seals, and He is about to take possession of the earth. So as He puts one foot upon the land and another upon the sea in verse 2, that symbolizes Christ taking possession of the world.

When Joshua was about to enter the Promised Land, God told him he would possess "every place that the sole of your foot shall tread upon" (Joshua 1:3). So when Christ puts one foot on the land and the other on the sea, it is a way of saying that everything belongs to Him. That only makes sense, because as Colossians 1:16 puts it, "By Him were all things created, that are in heaven, and that are in earth, visible and invisible, whether they be thrones, or dominions or principalities or powers: all things were created by him and for him." The Lamb who has broken the seals is now coming to take possession of the earth, and as He puts His feet on it, it is as though He is saying, "From end to end, pole to pole, to the ends of the earth, everything in this world belongs to me." He is coming not only to redeem souls, but to redeem creation.

His Message

He speaks with the roar of a lion (Revelation 10:3). Lions roar loudly to freeze their prey with fear. Jesus, who has been depicted as the Lamb of God, is also coming as the Lion of the tribe of Judah. He is coming to take vengeance upon His enemies.

A Startling Message

There are two sides to Christ's character. The Lamb offers comfort and peace. Without the Lamb side, you will never be saved. But there is also a Lion side, that brings tough judgment to His enemies. Not only is He Savior, He is King of Kings and Lord of Lords. His startling message is that He will roar as a mighty lion. The prophet Joel says, "The LORD also shall roar out of Zion and utter his voice from Jerusalem; and the heavens and the earth shall shake; but the LORD will be the hope of his people and the strength of the children of Israel" (Joel 3:16). The Lion of the tribe of Judah is about to deliver the people of Judah. He is going to roar as He comes to take vengeance upon a world that rejects our God and His Gospel. Jesus suffered in quietness as the Lamb, but soon He will roar as the Lion.

A Sealed Message

But part of His message is a secret. Thunder is used in the Bible as a symbol of God's voice. When He is about to judge the world, when the storm of His wrath is about to break, His voice thunders from the heavens as seven peals of thunder. Seven, God's perfect number, means that He has a powerful message. But we don't know what the message is, for the Lord orders it sealed up. It is too magnificent for description, and perhaps too terrifying. Just as God would not allow Paul to describe heaven after being caught up to it in 2 Corinthians 12, He will not allow John to reveal the message of the seven thunders. Don't let anybody try to tell you they know what that message is, for they don't. We will all find out one day at the end of time.

A Sure Message

But not only is His message startling and sealed, it is also a sure message. In verses 5 and 6 He lifts His hand and swears by Himself that these things will take place. The Lord takes an oath that these events will certainly happen. It might seem funny at first, God swearing upon Himself, but consider the concept of an oath. It is a promise made sure. In Hebrews we read, "When God made promises to Abraham, because he could swear by no greater: he sware by himself...for men verily swear by the greater: and an oath for confirmation is to them an end of all strife. Wherein God, willing more abundantly to show unto the heirs of promise the immutability of His counsel, confirmed it by an oath: that by two immutable things, in which it was impossible for God to lie, we might have a strong consolation" (Hebrew 6:13, 16-18). In other words, God looked around for something to swear by, and could find nothing greater than Himself. So He swore on Himself that He would keep His promises to Abraham. He is simply communicating that what He says will surely happen. If it does not happen, He would fail to be God. In essence, God is staking His very existence on His message.

A Solemn Message

The Lord Jesus says that there will no longer be such a thing as time (Revelation 10:6). This thing we call history is coming to a close. The world has had its chance; there can be no further delay. People have had every opportunity to repent, but even the judgments *of* God cannot bring them to turn from their evil ways. They gnash their teeth against God. They refuse His message and reject His Son. Time has run out for the inhabitants of the earth.

A Sweet Message

"But in the days of the voice of the seventh angel, when he shall begin to sound, the mystery of God should be finished, as he hath declared to his servants the prophets" (Revelation 10:7). When that seventh and last angel blows his trumpet, the mystery of God will be finished. That means one day very soon, mystery will turn to manifestation. Right now there are many things we do not know. It is as if we are looking through dark glass. But then we shall know God's plan fully.

As you look at our society, it seems that Satan is on a rampage. Wrong is on the throne and right is on the scaffold. There is much suffering and heartache in our world. People ask, "Why doesn't God do something about it?" Or they complain that He is too weak to do anything about it. But they fail to understand the mystery of God. The Lord is allowing the devil to have his way, but He has promised us that everything happening is part of His overall plan.

It is natural when things go badly in your life to ask the Lord, "Why?" But a better question to ask is, "How? How should I react to this, since I am sure it is the plan of God?" One day soon the mysteries of God are going to be finished. He will return in glory and take His people to be with Him in a land where there is no more pain or darkness or sickness or night. The sweetness of the message is that God has a plan, and that He is working His plan, and you are part of it. Rejoice that the Lord is coming soon and we will understand it all clearly.

> *And the voice which I heard from heaven spake unto me again, and said, Go and take the little book which is open in the hand of the angel which standeth upon the sea and upon the earth. And I went unto the angel, and said unto him, Give me the little book. And he said unto me, Take it, and eat it up; and it shall make thy belly bitter, but it shall be in thy mouth sweet as honey...and as soon as I had eaten it, my belly was bitter. And he said unto me, Thou must prophesy again before many peoples, and nations, and tongues, and kings.* (Revelation 10:8-11)

The message that Christ brings is comforting. It is "sweet in the mouth," as John puts it. But it is also a bitter message. It includes war and famine and death on a grand scale. It means the slaughter of billions of people. There is certainly no pleasure in that. The scroll that Jesus hands to John is full of such destruction that it makes the apostle sick. But he has been told to share the vision with everyone on earth, so that the good news of Christ will ring out and many will be saved. The sad part is that many will reject it, and will choose to separate themselves from God for eternity. That is indeed sad. But do you recognize the Good News in this? None of us deserves forgiveness. God in His great love and mercy has sent His own Son to die for us unworthy sinners. And that is indeed great news to be shared.

APPLICATION

1. What things have happened to you that have caused you to ask God, "Why? Why me?" Is it wrong to ask God that question? Is it wrong to grieve? Make sure to read John 11:32-38.

2. Take a look at Romans 8:26-27 and 12:15. Where does our comfort come from?

3. What principles for times of distress can you take from Psalm 46?

4. Some people think Christians should not be too emotional. What do the following Scriptures suggest:

   Psalm 5:1-3

Psalm 119:28

2 Samuel 6:12-15

Acts 20:36-38

Philippians 4:4

5. Why do we think the angel in Revelation 10 is Jesus Christ? What kind of message does He bring?

6. What would you say to someone who claimed to have "figured out" the secret message of the seven thunders in Revelation 10?

7. How is the story of Revelation good news? How is it a bitter pill?

8. As you study Philippians 4:4-9...what commands do you find? What comfort do you find? What promises do you find? What practical instructions do you find?

THE LIFE OF JOB

Do a mini-study on Job. When and where was Job written? Read Job 1:13-22. What happened? What was Job's response? Read Job 2:1-10. What happened? What was Job's response? Much of the book is a discussion between Job and his three friends, Eliphaz, Bildad, and Zophar. What is Eliphaz's main argument in Job 5:4-8 and 17-20? What about the cynical Bildad in 8:3-6? And the words of the argumentative old Zophar in 11:1-6? What does Job request in 13:3-6, 15-16 and 27:5-6? Sum up God's response in 38:1-4.

Chapter 13

GOD'S MIGHTY MESSENGERS

OVERVIEW

God will send two men to preach the truth to the world during the Tribulation Period. This chapter will explore the nature of those two men and their impact on the earth.

INTRODUCTION • REVELATION 11

A nd there was given to me a reed like unto a rod: and the angel stood, saying, Rise, and measure the temple of God, and the altar, and them that worship therein. But the court which is without the temple leave out, and measure it not; for it is given unto the Gentiles: and the holy city shall they tread underfoot forty and two months. (Revelation 11:1-2)

John continues to describe the events during the Tribulation Period, and now brings in some details to fill in the picture.

DISCUSSION

The prophet Daniel tells us that the Great Tribulation is going to last for seven years (Daniel 9:27). There will be a seven-year treaty signed between the Antichrist and Israel. He will rise, perhaps out of the European Common Market, and make a covenant to ensure the peace of Israel. He will allow the Jewish People to rebuild the temple. He will undoubtedly give them the materials and the wealth they will need. But Isaiah called this treaty "a covenant with death, and with hell are we at agreement; when the overflowing scourge shall pass through, it shall not come unto us: for we have made lies our refuge, and under falsehood have we hid ourselves" (Isaiah 28:15).

When the Antichrist enters into this covenant with the Jews, he will be received by the religious Jews because he allows them to rebuild the temple. He will be accepted by the political Jews because they will think that, at last, they have their freedom and safety assured. But right in the middle of this seven-year agreement, after three-and-one-half years, the Antichrist is going to move into the temple of God. According to 2 Thessalonians 2, he will declare himself God and demand worship. He will reach the ultimate aim of humanism. The Jews will fail to acknowledge him as God, and he will turn on them with unspeakable persecution. The next three-and-one-half years will be that "time of Jacob's trouble." Israel will know the greatest persecution it has ever experienced.

The Temple

During the Tribulation there is going to be a temple. At the time John wrote the Book of the Revelation, he knew that the temple in Jerusalem had been destroyed. But at some point in the future, there is going to be a new temple.

Some people want to argue over things like the temple in the Book of the Revelation. "Should we believe this to be a literal temple," they will ask, "or is this a symbol of something?" The best way to interpret Scripture is to take it literally as often as possible. If something is clearly a symbol, or if the author is using phenomenological language, then there is a symbolic meaning. But even symbolism does not do away with literal interpretation. We simply discover what the symbol stands for and believe it. Remember that we normally read books literally, and I would prefer the Lord one day chastise me for taking it too literally than for explaining too much of it away.

I believe the temple, the literal temple, is going to be rebuilt. It may be on the site where the Mosque of Omar, a sacred Muslim shrine, currently stands. Or it may be in another place. When Zerubbabel took the lead in rebuilding the temple, he created a place called a great synagogue to train young priests for Levitical service. The Jews still have a great synagogue where they train young men in the priestly function of the temple, so perhaps that will serve as the temple.

John is told to measure the temple of God and the altar, but he is not to measure the outer court. By this instruction, God is making a difference between those who know him and those who do not. There is going to be a division between those who truly worship Him and those who will not. The outer court is given to the Gentiles, and John is told they shall walk all over it for forty-two months, or three-and-one-half years.

The Two Witnesses

"And I will give power unto my two witnesses, and they shall prophesy a thousand two hundred and threescore days" (v. 3). These two witnesses are real people, not symbols. Some scholars have tried to say they stand for something, perhaps the Old and New Testament, but they are described as men who wear clothes, speak, perform miracles, and eventually die, their bodies lying in the street for all to see. God always works through men.

They Are Persons

No one knows who these two witnesses are. It is possible they are Moses and Elijah, come back from the dead. Verse 6 says they have the power to shut up the heavens and smite the earth with plagues, and Elijah and Moses did both of those things. These two men are going to come back from the other world and witness during the Great Tribulation. You may think it odd for two men to come back from the dead and give testimony, but Luke 9:30 says that these two characters have already come back to earth once, for Christ's transfiguration.

They Are Prophets

Verses 3, 6, and 10 tell us the witnesses will prophesy. They will be recognized as prophets of God. You know, in every age God has His prophet. He has always had His man. The 1,260 days that they prophesy is the same as the forty-two months that the Gentiles will be treading on the temple. It is also the same length of time spoken of in Daniel 12:7 and Revelation 12:14 when they refer to "time, times, and half a time" or three-and-one-half years. These two witnesses will prophecy for that length of time; then they will be killed for their message.

They Are Powerful

"And I will give power unto my two witnesses" (v. 3). These two men have incredible power, not just to prophesy, but to perform miracles. "These are the two olive trees, and the two candlesticks standing before the God of the earth. And if any man hurt them, fire proceedeth out of their mouth, and devoureth their enemies: and if any man will hurt them, he must in this manner be killed. These have power to shut heaven, that it rain not in the days of their prophecy: and have power over waters to turn them to blood, and to smite the earth with all plagues as often as they will" (vv. 4-6).

God calls the two witnesses olive trees and lampstands. The olive tree symbolizes fruit. The lampstand symbolizes light. And the two work together, for it is the oil of the olive that caused the lampstand to burn, and that oil is symbolic of the Holy Spirit. God's anointing will be upon these two witnesses.

They Are Persecuted

> *And when they shall have finished their testimony, the beast that ascendeth out of the bottomless pit shall make war against them, and shall overcome them, and kill them. And their dead bodies shall lie in the street of the great city, which spiritually is called Sodom and Egypt, where also our Lord was crucified. And they of the people and kindreds and tongues and nations shall see their dead bodies three days and an half, and shall not suffer their dead bodies to be put in graves. And they that dwell upon the earth shall rejoice over them, and make merry, and shall send gifts one to another; because these two prophets tormented them that dwelt on the earth. (vv. 7-10)*

God sends his two witnesses into the world to preach the truth, and they do just that. But the world can't stand the truth. When Christ came, they killed Him. When God sent the prophets, they were rejected. And these two witnesses will be killed, too, in the city of Jerusalem. But they will not be killed until they have finished the task God sent them to do. The man walking in the Spirit is immortal until his work is done. They killed Paul, but not until he said he had finished his course. They killed Jesus, but not until He could bow His head and say, "It is finished."

The Antichrist fights these two witnesses and puts them to death to the sound of great rejoicing. Perhaps it is this killing that catapults the Antichrist into worldwide fame and popularity. It will make him drunk with the sense of his own power and cause him to proclaim himself God. Up until this time, if anyone tried to harm the witnesses, fire came and killed the attackers. But the Antichrist is able to defeat them, causing rejoicing among all those who hate God and His Word. The people will not even bury their bodies; they just let them lie there in the street for all the world to see. And all the world *will* see— something that would not have been possible until the advent of satellite television. Everyone will be rejoicing, even sending presents to one another to celebrate, like an Antichristmas. These people must really hate God. His Word must be like a torment to their souls.

Things are so bad that Jerusalem is now totally corrupted. It is called Sodom because of its vice. It is called Egypt due to its vanity. And God is going to judge it because of its violence. It was here that Jesus was crucified. It is no longer the Holy City, but a hellish city.

They Are Preserved

The last thing to notice about God's mighty messengers is that they will be miraculously preserved by the Lord.

> *And after three days and an half, the Spirit of life from God entered into them and they stood upon their feet; and great fear fell upon them which saw them. And they heard a great voice from heaven saying unto them, Come up hither. And they ascended up to heaven in a cloud; and their enemies beheld them.* (vv. 11-12)

Imagine the scene: Envoys from around the world fly to Jerusalem to see the bodies. They are having a party, dancing in the street, giving gifts to one another, when suddenly the bodies stand up. Their bloated bodies return to normal size. They regain a healthy color. Their stiff limbs become pliable. They open their eyes and begin to breathe. And then, as everyone watches, a voice from heaven says, "Come up here," and the two witnesses ascend up to glory.

God's man is preserved. Though they put him to death, they cannot stop the message. What happens to these two will happen to all of us who love Jesus; we will rise again to join the Lord.

They Are Persuasive

These men loved God more than life itself. They were willing to die for their faith, and that made them persuasive to some people. Notice what verse 13 tells us: "And the same hour was there a great earthquake, and the tenth part of the city fell, and in the earthquake were slain of men seven thousand: and the remnant were affrighted, and gave glory to the God of heaven." In the end, God gets the glory for the lives of these two men. They were persuasive. They were men called by God, empowered, and faithful unto death.

Yet there were still many people who rejected the Lord. At the end of chapter 11, as the seventh angel blows his trumpet and Christ declares His dominion over all the world, there are still people angry with God. Rather than being relieved that the suffering is ending or repenting of their evil practices, "The nations were angry" (v. 18).

Our world wants to push you into its mold. They want you to believe that you need the biggest house, the best car, and the most money if you are to be successful. But God is not impressed with your earthly success. He is looking at your faithfulness. When God looks at my ministry as a pastor, He isn't interested in the size of my congregation, but the faithfulness of my life. The two witnesses were faithful unto death, and it made a difference in the lives of some people here on earth.

One day in the future, the temple of God will be opened in heaven (v. 19), and it will be a testimony to the faithfulness of our Lord.

APPLICATION

1. What interpretive principles should we keep in mind when reading Scripture?

2. What will be the significance of the new temple in Jerusalem?

3. Do a little research on the temple: Where was it? What was it used for? Why is it important to the Jews? What was the Holy of Holies? What were the other parts of the temple? When was the temple destroyed? What stands on the site of the old temple now?

4. What do you suppose the Lord means when He tells John in verse 2, "But the court which is without the temple leave out, and measure it not; for it is given unto the Gentiles"?

5. How do we know the witnesses were actual persons? How do we know they are not symbolic? What sort of power did they have? Why did God allow them to be killed?

6. What does Luke 21:12-19 teach us about living like the two witnesses?

7. Have you ever felt urged by the Lord to carry out an extremely difficult task? How did you respond? What was the result?

8. God is calling you to faithfulness. What do the following verses teach us about faithfulness?

   Luke 16:10-12

   1 Corinthians 1:9 and 10:13

   Galatians 5:22-23

   2 Thessalonians 3:1-5

   Hebrews 3:1-6

9. Who has made a big impact on your life because of his or her love and faithfulness toward Jesus Christ?

A LETTER TO MYSELF

Read Matthew 6:25-34. What are the underlying assumptions and basic truths of Jesus' teaching from the Sermon on the Mount? Take your thoughts and write them in a letter to yourself, encouraging and exhorting yourself to put those principles into practice.

Chapter 14

WHY SOME PEOPLE HATE THE JEWISH RACE

OVERVIEW

It seems that throughout history, someone has always been inciting violence against the Jews. Scripture gives a clear understanding of where that hate comes from and why it is evil.

INTRODUCTION • REVELATION 12

Some people just seem to hate the Jewish race. It is both evil and nonsensical, but some folks just want to blame the Jews for everything that has ever gone wrong in this world. A study of Revelation 12 will explain why some people share this ungodly, unjustified feeling of hatred for God's ancient people, the Jews.

DISCUSSION

> *There appeared a great wonder in heaven; a woman clothed with the sun, and the moon under her feet, and upon her head a crown of twelve stars: and she being with child cried, travailing in birth, and pained to be delivered.* (Revelation 12:1-2)

The Woman

In the very first verse of Revelation 12, we are introduced to a woman who is a symbol for something. When Scripture says, "There appeared a great wonder in heaven, a woman," the word for *wonder* is also translated "sign." This is a symbolic woman, so we have to determine what she stands for. Theologians have argued over what the symbolism means for ages. Catholics think she stands for Mary, but Mary gave birth to Christ on earth, not in heaven, so it is not Mary. Some think the woman represents the church, but the story in context does not fit the church. The founder of one cult movement even claimed to be the woman of Revelation 12 herself. The fact is, the woman of Revelation 12 represents the nation of Israel. She is called a sign and is described as being clothed with the sun and the moon, so she is not one real person. She has a crown of twelve stars, which represent the twelve tribes of Israel that have been made a royal nation by God. Israel is often referred to in Scripture as a woman. And she is a sign to all the nations that God can stoop to save the lowly and exalt the humble.

The woman mentioned is in childbirth, and she gives birth to Jesus Christ. That does not make the woman Mary, however, because the symbolic picture is that of the nation giving birth to a savior. In Isaiah 9:6 the prophet says, "Unto us a child is born." In a very real sense Jesus was the son of all Israel. That is why the writer to the Hebrews calls Christ "the seed of Abraham."

The Dragon

"And there appeared another wonder in heaven; and behold a great red dragon, having seven heads and ten horns and seven crowns upon his heads" (v. 3).

This is a depiction of the devil himself, as verse 9 makes very clear. He is red, the color of blood, and he is intent on bringing suffering to the woman and to the seed of the woman.

Jesus described the devil as a murderer in John 8:44, and here he is depicted as being perfectly evil. Notice that he has seven heads. The head in the Bible speaks of wisdom, and Satan is wise, though thoroughly corrupt. He also has ten horns, the symbol of power, and seven crowns, the symbol of authority. This dragon is an evil king, with great power and authority to carry out his murderous ways. Christ once called him the prince of this world, and that is a perfect description. He rules over this fallen world and makes himself out to be a king. But he is king of a dying planet winding down to judgment, and his subjects hate him for his rule.

Note what the next verse tells us: "And his tail drew the third part of the stars of heaven, and did cast them to the earth" (v. 4). Here John is not talking about literal stars, for there is no tail on earth long enough to knock stars from the sky. He is telling the story of Satan symbolically.

When Lucifer, the bright and morning star, desired to be like God, he was thrown out of heaven. He became the father of night, thoroughly evil and determined to battle the Lord God for control of the universe. At that time he convinced a third of the angels in heaven to join him, so a third of God's starry host fell with him. That means there are a great number of fallen spirit beings working as Satan's demonic force in the world today.

I once had the privilege of being in a prayer meeting with Leonard Ravenhill, the great British evangelist and author of *Why Revival Tarries*, and he prayed, "Lord, we read where one third of the angels fell from heaven, and praise God, that means two thirds didn't fall! It means there are two angels for every demon." Praise the Lord for helping us look on the bright side!

Satan has fallen angels to do his bidding, to serve as his emissaries. And John pictures him as lurking about, waiting for God's Son to be born so that He can be killed: "And the dragon stood before the woman which was ready to be delivered, for to devour her child as soon as it was born" (v. 4). It was Satan that inspired King Herod to murder all of those innocent babies in Bethlehem. The devil was trying to destroy the Lord Jesus when the mob attempted to seize Him in Luke 4. Satan even tried to trick Jesus into killing Himself by casting Himself down from the temple pinnacle. He has an ancient hatred for Israel and her seed, because they stand in the way of his being king forever on earth.

The Sovereign

"And she brought forth a man child, who was to rule all nations with a rod of iron: and her child was caught up unto God, and to His throne" (v. 5). That child, of course, is Jesus Christ. Psalm 2 tells us that He is going to rule over the nations with a rod of iron. The heathen, deceived by Satan, will rage against God, and the kings of the earth will scheme against His Son because they do not want Christ ruling over them. They hate Christ because He is good and holy and light cannot co-exist with darkness. They hate Israel because Israel is God's chosen race and Christ came out of that race. Remember the words of Jesus to His disciples: "If the world hate you, ye know that it hated me before it hated you. If ye were of the world, the world would love his own; but because ye are not of the world, but I have chosen you out of the world, therefore the world hateth you" (John 15:18-19).

So the heathen fight and rebel against the true King and His people. Yet in spite of all their rebellion and machinations, "I set my king upon my holy hill of Zion. I will declare the decree: the LORD hath said unto me, Thou art my Son; this day have I begotten thee. Ask of me, and I shall give thee the heathen for thine inheritance, and the uttermost parts of the earth for thy possession" (Psalm 2:6-8). The devil offered all of that to Jesus, but Christ knew that His Father had already promised it to Him. Christ will take back the earth, rule and reign over it. He will be caught up to God and take His throne. The resurrected Jesus is there on His throne in glory.

The Safety

"And the woman fled into the wilderness, where she hath a place prepared of God, that they should feed her there a thousand two hundred and threescore days" (v. 6). The Lord is going to prepare this woman who is so hated by her enemy, the devil. She will find a place of safety for three-and-one-half years, the last half of the Great Tribulation. In the middle of the Tribulation the Antichrist is going to come and sit in the temple of the Lord and claim to be God. The woman, Israel, will reject him as God and do battle over that claim.

In Matthew 24:15 Jesus referred to this event as "the abomination of desolation." It is the time when Satan does something so abominable it causes havoc in the land. "When ye therefore see the abomination of desolation…," Christ says, "flee into the mountains." It will be a sign that the terrible times are come upon Israel. The best thing to do is to hide. So God is going to protect a remnant of this nation the devil hates so much. God will preserve some of His people in Israel.

The War

> *And there was war in heaven: Michael and his angels fought against the dragon; and the dragon fought and his angels, and prevailed not; neither was their place found any more in heaven. And the great dragon was cast out, that old serpent, called the Devil, and Satan, which deceiveth the whole world: he was cast out into the earth, and his angels were cast out with him.* (Revelation 12:7-9)

One of the last places you would ever expect to find war is in heaven, but according to verse 7 a war is going to take place there. Many believers do not understand that Satan currently has access to heaven. Read the first two chapters in the book of Job, and you will see how Satan comes before God and accuses the brethren. He has access to heaven, and he also has access to earth. And there is a war going on between Satan and his demons and the angels of heaven. That is why in Revelation 20, the Lord creates a new heaven and a new earth. Even the heavens have been sullied by sin. Sin actually originated in heaven, when Lucifer rebelled against God. But Satan is going to be cast out of heaven. He will no longer have access to heaven or the ability to accuse. He has already fallen from his position as an exalted angel; soon he will be cast out of heaven entirely, and then he will be thrown into the bottomless pit. At the end of time Satan will be cast into the lake of fire. He is on his way down, all because he exalted himself.

Contrast Satan with Jesus, who humbled Himself and came down from heaven to save us. God brings low the exalted and exalts the lowly. Satan is on his way down; Christ is on His way up.

Satan is called a dragon because he is a strong, fierce opponent who wants to destroy you. He is also called a snake, a deceiver, and a devil, which means "a slanderer." Make no mistake: Satan is your enemy. He hates you and wants to harm you. He does all he can to deceive you, and he convinces much of the world to reject God. He is at war with God, so he makes war on Israel as a way to harm the Lord. Verse 17 tells us that Satan "went to make war with the remnant of her seed, which keep the commandments of God." The Antichrist will fight Israel, particularly those Jews who see the fulfillment of Scripture and turn to Jesus Christ. This will be Satan's way of attacking God.

The Overcomer

But God is going to win that war. "And I heard a loud voice saying in heaven, Now is come salvation, and strength, and the kingdom of our God, and the power of his Christ: for the accuser of our brethren is cast down, which accused them before our God day and night" (v. 10). Satan is the accuser, and Christ is our advocate. Satan will constantly be putting thoughts into your head about your failures, but Christ is there on your behalf. His Holy Spirit is there to correct you and keep you strong in the face of opposition. He can help you overcome Satan.

"And they overcame him by the blood of the Lamb, and by the word of their testimony; and they loved not their lives unto the death" (v. 11). God's people defeat Satan by (1) obtaining forgiveness through the shed blood of Jesus Christ at Calvary, (2) confessing their sin by making testimony to God, (3) committing their lives to Him, come what may. Jesus tells us, "Take courage; I have overcome the world." Paul encourages us to "not be overcome by evil, but overcome evil with good." As Christians, we are overcomers. And we defeat Satan when we live our lives for Jesus Christ.

The Woe

"Therefore rejoice, ye heavens, and ye that dwell in them. Woe to the inhabiters of the earth and of the sea! for the devil is come down unto you, having great wrath, because he knoweth that he hath but a short time" (v. 12). The devil can sense his coming doom. He is going to be like a cornered animal, fighting with all his might to defeat God and His people. At that time he will enter into the body of the Antichrist. That man, considered a great world leader, will suddenly become the devil incarnate. Satan will fill that man with such malevolence and malignant hate that he will move into the temple of the Jews and demand to be worshipped as their God.

"And when the dragon saw that he was cast unto the earth, he persecuted the woman which brought forth the man child" (v. 13). The devil hates the Jewish people because their race brought the

Savior into this world. That Savior spells the demise of Satan. That Lamb will slay the dragon. And heaven will cheer.

APPLICATION

1. In your own words, why do so many people hate the Jews? What do you think is behind the virulent, anti-Israeli feeling in the Middle East?

2. How do we know the woman in Revelation 12 is a symbol for Israel? How do we know her son is the Messiah, Jesus Christ?

3. Take a look at the following verses to discover truths about Satan: Isaiah 14:12-15 and Revelation 12:3, 4, 9, 10, 13, 17. What are his names? Where does he come from? What did he do? What is his task and his motivation on earth? What will be his ultimate end?

4. In contrast, what do the following passages teach us about Jesus Christ: John 1:1-3, 10-14 and Philippians 2:5-11. What are His names? Where does He come from? What did He do? What is His task and His motivation on earth? What will be His ultimate end?

5. How does Satan usually accuse you? How can you tell the difference between Satan's accusations and the Holy Spirit's promptings in your life?

6. Read Ephesians 6:10-20. Who are we fighting? What are we to take into battle? What protects us? What offensive weapons do we use? In your own words, how do we fight that spiritual battle with Satan?

7. A short study of Matthew 24 will bring Christ's own words to bear on your understanding of the end times. In verses 1-8, what does Jesus say will be happening in the world at that time? According to Matthew 24:9-14, what further events will occur? What is Jesus referring to in verse 15? What does he suggest people do about it in verses 16-28? What is the lesson of verses 29-35? What does Christ tell us in verses 36-41? Finally, what does the Lord encourage us to do in verses 42-51?

THE KING

Read Psalm 2, then write an acrostic poem using the word "kingdom." Have the first word start with the letter "K," the second with "I," etc. Your poem does not have to rhyme.

Chapter 15

THE BEAST OUT OF THE SEA

OVERVIEW

Revelation 13 is a most interesting study of the Antichrist. We will find out his history and his plan for controlling the world.

INTRODUCTION • REVELATION 13

And I stood upon the sand of the sea, and saw a beast rise up out of the sea, having seven heads and ten horns, and upon his horns ten crowns, and upon his heads the name of blasphemy" (Revelation 13:1). So John begins his description of the Antichrist, a beast lurking in the shadows of history and awaiting his time on earth.

DISCUSSION

The Advent of the Beast

Just as our Lord Jesus Christ has an advent, so does the Antichrist. The sea in this passage represents the nations of the world. They are in turmoil, with governments seething and changing. Isaiah says that the wicked are like the troubled sea that cannot rest. Later in Revelation John is told, "The waters which thou sawest, where the horse sitteth, are peoples, and multitudes, and nations, and tongues" (Revelation 17:15), and out of this turmoil of individuals comes the Antichrist.

As you look at the confused world situation today, you can see the fulfillment of Biblical prophecy. Europe is becoming more of a federation than a collection of separate states. The Soviet Union has fallen apart but is recreating itself as the new, powerful Russia. Iran and Iraq are in turmoil, like so much of the Middle East, and so is the old Hungary/Serbia area that has already led to two World Wars. Much of this area could fall under Russian influence, just as the prophet foretold in Ezekiel 30, and there has long been a sense of foreboding that Russia will turn against Israel.

If you look to the Far East, you will see the great red dragon of communist China, with her 200 million soldiers, eyeing Mongolia and eastern Russia for herself. There is continuing trouble with Korea, and Japanese nationalism is again on the rise.

Finally, in the land of Israel we find the lion of Judah sharpening her claws, expecting war at every turn of events. The Israelis now have nuclear capability, and we can expect them to use it if they deem it necessary. All of these nations, like the billowing ocean with its constant seething and motion, will lead us to a place where we embrace the Beast. The perilous times prophesied in Scripture have come. Christians need to know the situation, know how to pray, and know how to lead men to Christ in the midst of it all. The proof that you understand Bible prophecy is not that you go around getting into philosophical debates about arcane theological topics, but that you tell someone about the Savior of the world. The coming events cast shadows ahead of time to what the Bible calls the "beginning of sorrows." I believe we are experiencing those first sorrows now, and we need to prepare those around us for the coming of Jesus Christ.

If you don't know what will happen, you will have headline hysteria. You will be in constant consternation. But when you know what is coming, you can take comfort in the fact that God has a plan for the world. When you know that the Bible has already prophesied these things, you can praise God that it is just as He said it would be. We cannot afford to be ignorant because we are living in the last days.

The Ancestry of the Beast

John "saw a beast rise up out of the sea, having seven heads and ten horns, and upon his horns, ten crowns, and upon his heads the name of blasphemy. And the beast which I saw was like unto a leopard, and his feet were as the feet of a bear, and his mouth as the mouth of a lion: and the dragon gave him his power, and his seat, and great authority" (Revelation 13:1-2). If there was ever a man whose father was the devil, this is the man. His ancestry goes right back to the devil.

Family Likeness

Notice that the Beast is described as having seven heads and ten horns. If you go back to Revelation 12:3, you will see Satan described as "a great red dragon, having seven heads and ten horns, and seven crowns upon his head." As you read the description of the Beast in chapter 13, you will see the family likeness. There is no mistaking who his father is. When Jesus walked this earth He said, "He who has seen me has seen the Father." Christ was the exact representation of His Father. You could see God by looking at His Son. When the Beast comes, who is the Antichrist and the false messiah, he will be able to say, "He that hath seen me has seen my father," for the Beast will be the visible expression of the invisible devil. He will say, as Jesus said, "I and my father are one," for he will be the representative of his evil father on earth. You can see the family likeness. He has seven heads, representing full knowledge, and ten horns, which represent the ten nation confederacy of Europe prophesied in Scripture; the revived Roman Empire.

The Family Lineage

Notice that the Beast is described as a lion, a bear, and a leopard. I believe these all stand for past world empires. In Daniel 7 there is an outline of world history which describes all of these. The lion was the kingdom of Babylon, the bear was the Medo-Persian empire, and the leopard was ancient Greece under Alexander the Great. And Scripture tells us that this beast is going to be like that ancient lion, that bear, and that leopard. The Antichrist is going to inherit the beastly characteristics of those three kingdoms. The world that rejected the Lamb and Lord is going to receive the devil and beast.

Jesus once said, "I am come in my Father's name, and ye receive me not: If another shall come in his own name, him ye will receive" (John 5:43). They rejected the spotless Lamb, but will accept the spotted beast. They will receive the bear with his ugly claws, the lion with his ravenous mouth, and the cunning leopard with his desire to conquer and kill. That is the family lineage of the Beast, and he will be true to those who have gone before him.

The Family Legacy

In verse 2, John gives us the detail that "the dragon gave him his power, and his seat, and great authority." The dragon is Satan, and he plans to leave his son, the Antichrist, a legacy of great power. Paul tells us in 2 Thessalonians 2:9 that the man of sin will come "with all power and signs and lying wonders." Just as the Holy Spirit empowered the Lord Jesus Christ, the unholy spirit will empower the Antichrist. He will receive his power from the devil himself. The reason the Antichrist, if he is alive today, does not have full power is because he is restrained by the Holy Spirit. But one day that restraining force will be taken out of the way. Then the man of sin will be revealed. He will be turned loose on the world with all his lying power and false wonders. He will make the world believe that evil is good, that black is white, and that up is down. And he will be given power to control the world.

The Appeal of the Beast

You might think that an evil master like this would have no appeal. But look at Revelation 13:3: "And I saw one of his heads, as it were wounded to death; and his deadly wound was healed: and all the world wondered after the beast."

The Antichrist will be quite a man in the eyes of the world. When you see the biblical term "beast," do not mistake that to mean someone hideous. The term refers to character, not appearance. Even the devil himself, who is a wicked dragon, appears to people as an angel of light. I personally think the Antichrist will be handsome, witty, and charming. He will obviously be intelligent. The reason for his immense popularity will be wrapped up in something that is going to happen to him. He is going to receive a deadly wound in the head and then be resuscitated. That will be a satanic imitation of the resurrection of Jesus Christ.

It is strange how a man's popularity can be enhanced by an event like this. President Kennedy's popularity went way up after he was assassinated. The same happened to President Reagan after the attempt on his life. A few years ago when someone tried to shoot the Pope, he lived and the whole world wondered after him. That is what will happen to the Antichrist. It will seem like a miracle, and the whole world will wonder after him. He will seem to be a marvel, and because of his grave injury he will be granted respect and will claim to speak for peace. He will appear as the world's benefactor.

The Ambition of the Beast

"And they worshipped the dragon which gave power unto the beast: and they worshiped the beast, saying, Who is like unto the beast? who is able to make war with him?" (v. 4). The Antichrist's first ambition is to deify himself. He wants to be worshipped. Second Thessalonians tells us that he is going to sit in the temple of God, showing himself to be God. You may wonder if people will believe that a man is God, but our world is full of those claiming a unique relationship with God. In China, millions worship Mao Tse Tung. In the 1940's the German people worshipped Hitler. And right here in America, we have all sorts of swamis and cult leaders who have convinced some poor souls that they are divine. It has always been Satan's desire to be worshipped.

The Antichrist also wants to defy God. "And there was given unto him a mouth speaking great things and blasphemies; and power was given unto him to continue forty and two months. And he opened his mouth in blasphemy against God, to blaspheme his name, and his tabernacle, and them that dwell in heaven" (vv. 5-6). The Antichrist is going to hate the Rapture, so he will think of some lie that is so clever it will deceive people into thinking we have been taken out as God's judgment against us. He cannot touch God, so he will be reduced to name-calling.

He will also seek to destroy the saints: "And it was given unto him to make war with the saints, and to overcome them" (v. 7). After the Rapture of the church, when 144,000 Jews and many Gentiles come to trust Christ as their personal Savior, the Antichrist will pour out his venom and hatred against believers. New Christians are going to face torture and terror as the Beast becomes drunk on the blood of the saints.

Not only that, but he will also seek to dominate the nations of the world. "And power was given him over all kindreds, and tongues, and nations. And all that dwell upon the earth shall worship him, whose names are not written in the book of life of the Lamb slain from the foundation of the world" (vv. 7- 8). He will have global control, unifying the world with one world government. He will do it by dazzling some, dominating others, and murdering a few to get his way. He will be the christ of the cults, the god of the ungodly. He will be worshipped in the earth because he is going to delude the masses.

The Agent of the Beast

"And I beheld another beast coming up out of the earth; and he had two horns like a lamb, and he spake as a dragon" (v. 11). The Antichrist has a helper or press secretary who is a deceiver. He speaks with the voice of Satan. He is the anti-spirit, and just as the Holy Spirit's role is to draw us close to Christ, the work of this counterfeiter will be to make the dragon attractive to those who do not yet know him: "And he exerciseth all the power of the first beast before him, and causeth the earth and them which dwell therein to worship the first beast, whose deadly wound was healed" (v. 12).

The Antichrist will be a master of miracles: "And he doeth great wonders, so that he maketh fire come down from heaven on the earth in the sight of men, and deceiveth them that dwell on the earth by the means of those miracles which he had power to do in the sight of the beast"(vv. 13-14). He will be able to make fire come from the heavens, perhaps a reference to nuclear power that will make everyone knuckle under to the Antichrist's leadership.

He will also encourage the worship of the Beast, "saying to them that dwell on the earth, that they should make an image of the beast, which had the wound by a sword, and did live. And he had power to give life unto the image of the beast, that the image of the beast should both speak, and cause that as many as would not worship the image of the beast should be killed" (vv. 14-15). This may simply be a television image that is beamed to everyone's home, or it might be some sort of computer image that everyone receives.

> And he causeth all, both small and great, rich and poor, free and bond, to receive a mark in their right hand, or in their foreheads: and that no man might buy or sell, save he that had the mark, or the name of the beast, or the number of his name. Here is wisdom. Let him that hath understanding count the number of

the beast: for it is the number of a man; and his number is Six hundred threescore and six. (vv. 16-18)

Everyone will be given a mark. Without it, people will not be able to buy or sell. This is the start of the cashless society, a way to control every person. It will seem so reasonable and simple and necessary. No one will carry cash, it will cut down on crime, and, unfortunately, it will allow the world leader to turn the entire planet into one giant concentration camp. Satan will be running things, trying to be God. But try as he may, he always comes up short. God is a seven. Satan works hard but always is merely a 666—a cheap imitation of God.

APPLICATION

1. Why is it a good idea to study the details of the Revelation? What should it motivate us to do? In your life, what difference does this study make?

2. How is the world situation like the sea in Revelation 13:1? What world situations make you believe the end of the world could be coming soon?

3. Read 2 Thessalonians 2. What is Paul's encouragement to us in verses 1-4? What do verses 5-8 reveal about why the Antichrist doesn't seize control today? What do verses 9-12 reveal about the Antichrist and the people who follow him? What, then, is our motivation in verses 13-17?

4. In Revelation 13:2, what does the bear represent? How is the Antichrist like the bear? What does the lion represent? How is the Antichrist like that lion? What does the leopard represent? Why is that a particularly appropriate reference to the Antichrist?

5. What is the source of the Antichrist's power? If the word *seat* were translated "throne" in verse 2, what does that signify?

6. Why do you suppose all the world submits to the Beast?

7. What does John warn us about in 1 John 2:18? Restate 1 John 2:19 in your words. What does 1 John 2:22-23 reveal about the Antichrist?

8. What does Revelation 13:6 suggest will happen in response to the Rapture?

9. Explain your understanding of Revelation 13:10?

10. Why is the second beast (v. 11) an anti-spirit? Define his role?

THE MARK OF THE BEAST

Scientists are already experimenting with implanting computer chips on foreheads or the backs of hands (the two easiest spots to expose in cold weather climates). If this system could be put in place to create a banking system with your financial information on your computer chip, how could that system limit your ability to buy and sell? How would it give government more control of your life?

Chapter 16

THE MARK OF
THE BEAST

OVERVIEW

In Revelation 13 there are some details about the "mark of the beast," the system that the Antichrist will use to control the world. In this study we will explore his mark and his number, 666.

INTRODUCTION • REVELATION 13

We live in amazing times. In our lifetimes we have seen the atom split, space explored, and the world linked through satellite communication. We have seen Israel restored as a nation, just as was prophesied, and the rebirth of the old Roman Empire as the European Common Market. We have all watched the advent of the computer age and the proliferation of electronic banking, and the day is coming when we will have a cashless society, when every man and woman will work, buy, and sell using numbers and bar codes. We have seen a tremendous explosion of knowledge, as the Prophet Daniel predicted when he said, "Even to the time of the end many shall run to and fro, and knowledge shall be increased."

Daniel says that one of the ways we can know we are living in the last days is that people are frantically crossing the globe searching for information. We used to travel on horseback, taking all day to get from one town to another. Now we travel on airplanes at 2,000 miles an hour, or we use satellite links that instantly relay information to us from around the world. Scientists tell us that our information doubles every few years. Seventy percent of the medicines we use today have been developed since World War II. Ninety percent of all scientists who have ever lived are alive right now. Knowledge is increasing at a fantastic rate. All of this increase in knowledge is taking us someplace, and I fear it will be soon.

DISCUSSION

And I beheld another beast coming up out of the earth; and he had two horns like a lamb, and he spake as a dragon. And he exerciseth all the power of the first beast before him, and causeth the earth and them which dwell therein to worship the first beast, whose deadly wound was healed. And he doeth great wonders, so that he maketh fire come down from heaven on the earth in the sight of men, and deceiveth them that dwell on the earth by the means of those miracles which he had power to do in the sight of the beast; saying to them that dwell on the earth, that they should make an image to the beast, which had the wound by a sword, and did live. And he had power to give life unto the image of the Beast, that the image of the beast should both speak, and cause that as many as would not worship the image of the beast should be killed. And he causeth all, both small and great, rich and poor, free and bond, to receive a mark in their right hand, or in their foreheads: and that no man might buy or sell, save he that had the mark, or the name of the beast, or the number of his name. Here is wisdom. Let him that hath understanding count the number of the beast: for it is the number of a man: and his number is Six hundred threescore and six. (Revelation 13:11-18)

The False Prophet

Just as there is a holy Trinity, there is also an unholy trinity. Satan is the evil father; the beast is his son, the Antichrist, and the false prophet is the anti-spirit. This prophet is a sinister minister of propaganda for the Antichrist, making him look good to the world.

Servant of Satan

The false prophet has two horns, so he seems harmless. He looks like a lamb. But don't be fooled. He speaks like a dragon, like Satan himself. He is the servant of Satan, who gave him his start. Scripture says he comes up out of the earth, as opposed to the Antichrist, who comes from the mass of humanity called "the sea." Coming from the earth may mean he comes from the land of Palestine. He might be an apostate Jew who serves as the enforcer for the Antichrist.

The Worker of Worship

The false prophet's role is to get people to worship the Antichrist . The devil isn't opposed to worship; he thinks worship is fine. Witchcraft, the occult, spiritism, astrology, and new age thinking all tell us of Satan's desire to be worshipped. He isn't opposed to religion. Man is inherently religious, and the devil uses man's nature against him. When man refuses to worship the God who became a man, they are tricked into worshipping the man who claims to be God. "For such are false apostles, deceitful workers, transforming themselves into the apostles of Christ. And no marvel; for Satan himself is transformed into an angel of light. Therefore it is no great thing if his ministers also be transformed as the ministers of righteousness; whose end shall be according to their works" (2 Corinthians 11:13-15). When the false prophet appears, he will not appear as something hideous, but as someone kind, righteous, and good. He will convince people to worship the Beast.

Master of Miracles

The false prophet will do great wonders and miracles to prove his authority. He will make fire come down from heaven. We don't know if that is actual fire like Elijah called down from heaven, or if this is a reference to his authority to control weapons from space. But he will be able to prove his power through miracles.

Make no mistake, Satan can work miracles. Just as Elijah brought fire from heaven, the devil can imitate that miracle. When God turned Moses' rod into a snake, Pharoah's magicians turned their rods into snakes. He has a dark, unholy power in this world. Revelation 16 tells us that demonic spirits work miracles for the kings of the earth. Christ once warned that in the last days "there shall arise false Christs, and false prophets, and shall show great signs and wonders; insomuch that, if it were possible, they shall deceive the very elect" (Matthew 24:24). You cannot tell if a man is from God just because he performs some miraculous sign. So if people rely on their natural wisdom, they will be deceived. Don't fool yourself into believing that you could never be taken in by the Antichrist. He can fool the best.

Deuteronomy 13:1-3 explains why the Lord allows Satan to have miraculous powers:

> *If there arise among you a prophet, or a dreamer of dreams, and giveth thee a sign or a wonder, and the sign or wonder come to pass, whereof he spake unto thee saying, Let us go after other gods, which thou hast not known, and let us serve them; thou shalt not hearken unto the words of that prophet, or that dreamer of dreams: for the LORD your God proveth you, to know whether ye love the LORD your God with all your heart and with all your soul.*

God will allow a false prophet to perform a wonder so that it might serve as a test, to see if the people will chase after some other god. A miracle is simply a sign attesting to the power of the one performing it. The miracles of Jesus attest to His mighty power. The signs of Satan attest to his power. So a sign or miracle may be a witness, or it may serve as a warning. You make a grave mistake by building your faith on signs and wonders. It is far better for you to build your faith on Scripture. Christ warned people that it was an evil generation who merely wanted more and more miracles as proof of His deity. Don't let your spiritual life focus on signs. Let it focus on the Word of God.

Do you remember the story in John 4:47-48 where Jesus healed the nobleman's son? "When he heard that Jesus was come out of Judaea into Galilee, he went unto him and besought him that he would come down, and heal his son: for he was at the point of death. Then said Jesus unto him, Except ye see signs and wonders, ye will not believe" (vv. 47-48). What a startling rebuke our Lord gave to a man asking for his son's life! But Jesus knew of the evil proclivity in this man's heart. So after being rebuked, the nobleman spoke to Jesus with a different spirit: "Sir, come down ere my child die. Jesus saith unto him, Go thy way; thy son liveth. And the man believed the word that Jesus had spoken unto him, and he went his way" (vv. 49-50). A change came upon that man. He "believed the word" of Jesus. There was contrast to his earlier appeal. He was no longer asking for a sign or wonder, but for the Word of God.

It is also instructive to consider that that nobleman did not rush home. He was near his home enough to get there in a few hours, but he stayed in the area to hear Jesus. Not until he saw his servants did he learn that his son had been healed at the very time Christ spoke the words, "Thy son liveth." And John records, "So the father knew that it was at the same hour, in the which Jesus said unto him, Thy son liveth: and himself believed, and his whole house" (v. 53). That nobleman was transformed because of the words of Jesus Christ. He didn't have to see a sign. He didn't even have to go home to check and see that Christ had miraculously healed his boy. He simply trusted Jesus' words. That is the example we should follow.

The Controller of Commerce

The false prophet will not only work miracles and encourage worship of the Antichrist, he will enforce his regime through computer controlled numbers. He will put marks on the forehead or hand of every person, so as to know all about each one. That mark of the Beast is the evil counterpart to the work of God. When a Christian is saved he receives the seal of the Spirit, which marks him as God's child. The devil's children will be branded by the Beast as a seal that they belong to the Antichrist. That is the mark of the beast, put on all people as a way to make them part of the world's economic system.

What is this brand of hell? The Bible says it is wrapped up in the numbers six, six, six. Six is the number of man; three is the number of God, so three sixes are man making himself into God. We don't know just how Satan will use this number, although people have had all sorts of guesses. For example, during President Reagan's term I heard Christians say that his full name, Ronald Wilson Reagan, contained the right number of letters, 666. But so does my name, Adrian Pierce Rogers, so I don't think they've figured it all out yet! We don't know just what the numbers mean, but we do know how the system will work.

It will control the world's commerce. Let me give an example. On the back of your credit cards are magnetic strips that contain information in a series of numbers that can be read by a computer. Soon you will never have to write another check, or keep cash in your billfold, or buy a stamp. It will be easy to do and much safer than carrying around cash. Let's say that every purchase you make is done by this system. A thief wouldn't be able to steal your money because he couldn't get to it, nor would he be able to sell it because he wouldn't have access to your numbers. Europe already has a system in place for large corporations to do business this way, and soon it will be the norm for everyone. The "universal product code" on all packaging is one form of this system, and your automatic payroll deposit from your job is another. And pretty soon you will be able simply to wave your hand under that light beam at the supermarket, and they'll have the proper amount deducted from your account.

It all sounds so reasonable, and any computer expert will tell you it is technologically possible right now. Your bank can automatically pay your mortgage and utility bills, and the government can electronically monitor your income and do your taxes for you. The government is computerizing everything, and they are pushing for national identity cards and one super credit card per person. There is a mounting concern over the government using computers to control, intimidate, and harass the citizenry. They will have all kinds of information on you, and an evil government could use it against you.

The scariest part of all this is what is known as "plastic surgery"—not the cosmetic kind, but the financial kind. In the future, the enforcement of financial obligations will present few difficulties because failure to pay your debts could be disastrous. You could be cut off from your bank cards, making you a non-person, unable to buy or sell. The false prophet will set up a system where everyone, small and great, is forced to become part of this economic system to survive. Everyone will require the mark of the beast just to survive. In instituting this system, the false prophet will help the Antichrist attain world domination.

APPLICATION

1. Draw a timeline for your life. What year were you born? What significant scientific events have occurred in your lifetime? What significant political events? What significant historical events? What technological changes have occurred? What have been the cultural (music, art, literature) milestones? How has daily life changed?

2. What do we know for certain about the false prophet?

3. Compare the role of the false prophet with the role of the Holy Spirit. Read Revelation 13:11-18, John 16:5-16, and Romans 8:1-17.

	False Prophet	**Holy Spirit**
Who sent him		
What is his task		
Whom he glorifies		
What he brings		
What is the result		

4. What does Romans 8:18-27 reveal about the role of the Holy Spirit in our lives?

5. How can the false prophet appear harmless but actually be harmful? Are you often fooled by appearances? When was a time you were badly mistaken about someone's character?

6. The false prophet will coerce people into worshipping the Antichrist. Do you see anyone being worshipped in our culture? What form does that worship take? What does Jesus teach us in Matthew 4:10?

7. Can Satan perform signs and wonders? How can we know who is behind them? What is the problem with becoming involved with signs and wonders? What should our focus be, if not signs and wonders?

THE HOLY SPIRIT

Look up the New Testament references to the Holy Spirit in a concordance. What are the promises made in Scripture about what the Holy Spirit does for us?

www.ingramcontent.com/pod-product-compliance
Lightning Source LLC
Chambersburg PA
CBHW052008090426
42741CB00008B/1598